Charlotte Lydia Riley is a historian of twentieth-century Britain at the University of Southampton, specialising in questions about empire, politics, culture and identity. She is editor of *The Free Speech Wars* and author of *Imperial Island: A History of Empire in Modern Britain*. Her writing has appeared in a wide range of publications including the *Guardian*, *New Statesman*, *Washington Post* and *History Today*. She tweets @lottelydia.

Is Free Speech Under Threat?

CHARLOTTE LYDIA RILEY

THE BODLEY HEAD
LONDON

1 3 5 7 9 10 8 6 4 2

The Bodley Head, an imprint of Vintage, is part of the
Penguin Random House group of companies whose addresses
can be found at global.penguinrandomhouse.com

First published by the Bodley Head in 2024

penguin.co.uk/vintage

Typeset in 13.3/18.2pt Calluna by Jouve (UK), Milton Keynes
Printed and bound in Great Britain by Clays Ltd, Elcograf S.p.A.

The authorised representative in the EEA is Penguin Random House
Ireland, Morrison Chambers, 32 Nassau Street, Dublin D02 YH68

A CIP catalogue record for this book is available from the British Library

ISBN 9781847928221

Penguin Random House is committed to a sustainable future
for our business, our readers and our planet. This book is
made from Forest Stewardship Council® certified paper.

Is Free Speech Under Threat?

In July 2020, a letter appeared on the website of *Harper's* magazine which sparked a fierce debate.[1] Organised by the writer Thomas Chatterton Williams, 'A Letter on Justice and Open Debate' was signed by 152 writers, academics and journalists. In it, these signatories argued that American cultural institutions were facing 'a moment of trial' which saw the right to free speech under threat. In the context of protests for 'racial and social justice', they argued that a 'new set of moral attitudes and political commitments' had arisen in America. But rather than leading to greater freedoms – as might be expected from revolutionary movements for equality – these attitudes and commitments had instead weakened American 'norms of open debate and toleration of differences', creating 'ideological conformity'. The letter particularly condemned

I

those who, through their opposition to the authoritarianism of Donald Trump and his supporters, had ironically embraced their 'own brand of dogma and coercion' by creating an 'intolerant climate' on 'all sides' of the political spectrum. They were referring, of course, to 'cancel culture'. The authors warned that this created a 'stifling atmosphere' that would ultimately harm progressive causes; instead of seeking to shut down speech that was deemed morally or politically beyond the pale, people should 'defeat bad ideas' through debate. Only through 'exposure, argument, and persuasion' could 'bad ideas' be vanquished.

The '*Harper's* letter' certainly provoked debate. One piece in the *New York Times* approvingly argued that the letter illuminated newsroom discussions in which 'demands [for diversity and inclusion] – and the social media dynamics that propel them – go too far'.[2] But many disagreed, and the signatories also faced a wave of criticism. (In *Tablet*, Paul Berman wrote that the letter, which he had signed, was 'a fine example of a self-verifying manifesto'; the backlash it provoked, he claimed, served to demonstrate 'the reality of what it points out'.[3] The *Daily Telegraph* agreed, decrying the letter's 'vicious' aftermath and claiming that 'repercussions' from its publication had led to the resignation of one of its signatories.[4])

Much of the backlash took aim at the letter's premise and disputed the existence of the 'stifling' intolerance that it claimed to identify. But it was also concerned specifically by the identities of the signatories, and their personal stakes in this debate that perhaps clouded their judgement. For instance, the *Daily Beast* ran a piece bluntly entitled 'J.K. Rowling and Other Assorted Rich Fools Want to Cancel "Cancel Culture"'.[5] For many critics, it was impossible to separate Rowling's signature from her high-profile 'gender critical' position, for which they believed she had received legitimate criticism. One piece in *Glamour* magazine addressed J. K. Rowling directly, proclaiming that 'it's not "cancel culture" that's led to people withdrawing their support from you, here's what has . . .', before criticising the writer's 'transphobic opinions'. The article also pointed out that there was little sense in which Rowling's body of work, still wildly commercially successful, had actually been 'cancelled'.[6]

Another signatory, Ian Buruma, had resigned from his position as editor of the *New York Review of Books* two years previously after being criticised for publishing an essay by Jian Ghomeshi, in which Ghomeshi characterised accusations against himself of sexual assault and harassment as 'inaccurate'.[7] But was Buruma a victim of 'cancel culture', or simply an editor who had been forced to take responsibility for an unpopular editorial decision and thus been held accountable for a professional misstep? When the signatories of the *Harper's* letter claimed that a culture of censorship had 'steadily narrow[ed] the boundaries of what can be said without the threat of reprisal' and that there must be 'room for experimentation, risk taking, and even mistakes', it sounded to their critics like they were asking for a world wherein they didn't have to face any consequences for what they had said, written or published. But, as the subheading on the *Daily Beast* piece about J. K. Rowling stated plainly, 'people disagreeing with you is not the same as censorship or cancellation'.

The *Harper's* letter conflated two different forms of censorship in its assertion that 'restriction of debate, whether by a repressive government or an intolerant society, invariably hurts those who lack power and makes everyone less capable of democratic participation'. No one would dispute that repressive governments pose real legal and political threats to writers and thinkers, enjoying as they do the full power of the state to intimidate and control their citizens. But even if we accept the premise that democratic nations such as the UK and USA have become 'intolerant societies', making it hard for writers to flourish, the punishments that citizens can exert on one another are of an entirely different order to that of government repression. Lumping governments and societies together like this muddies the water, and perhaps makes the stakes seem much higher than they actually are.

As critics pointed out, the letter also prioritised an idealised form of free speech above all other concerns: it seemed 'to be suggesting that all viewpoints should be published in opinion pages, with no limits on what those viewpoints might be', and it had been quick to write off significant and troubling cultural issues, such as institutional racism in the workplace, as 'clumsy mistakes'.[8] In this way, the letter's authors appeared to have constructed a reality in which all speech should be given the benefit of the doubt, and in which all opposition to free speech is therefore illegitimate. All criticism was defined as illiberal. All pushback was censorship.

The *Harper's* letter had aimed to bring people together from across the political spectrum. As Deirdre Nansen McCloskey, a trans woman, wrote, 'many and diverse people are worried by group-thinkers who won't listen' to the other side of debates.[9] And yet, as critics of the letter pointed out, the *Harper's* signatories were mostly 'white, wealthy' and, crucially, 'prominent people with huge platforms complaining they don't have enough latitude to share their views' in one of the most prestigious magazines in the country: 'The irony of the piece is that nowhere in it do the signatories mention how marginalized voices have been silenced for generations in journalism, academia, and publishing.'[10] In other words, the precarity and anxiety that the authors of the *Harper's* letter were expressing were not new: they were the conditions that powerless and oppressed people have had to endure throughout history. The only distinction was that most people have not had the opportunity to publish their concerns about this in a respected magazine for everyone to read.

The *Harper's* letter did not come out of the blue. It was part of a wave of cultural concern and charged debate about intolerance and censoriousness that had been building for some years in the United

Kingdom and the United States – both countries that consider themselves bastions of free speech. The US has its First Amendment, which guarantees its citizens the rights to freedom of speech, freedom of religion, a free press and freedom of assembly; the UK has state-sanctioned 'British values' that espouse respect for democracy, tolerance and freedom of speech alongside the rule of law.[11] Both countries are proud of their free press and lack of state censorship, and have frequently framed foreign policy interventions as attempts to defend and foster these values throughout the world. And yet there has been, in recent years, a pervasive transatlantic anxiety that we live in a new age of censoriousness, in which free speech is increasingly under threat. As the *Harper's* letter demonstrated, this perceived threat comes not from states and governments but from a youthful, moralising movement associated with the politically progressive, 'woke' left: younger millennials and Generation Z, catalysed by activism such as #MeToo, the trans rights movement, and Black Lives Matter.[12]

This essay argues that, broadly speaking, the *Harper's* letter was wrong and its critics were right. Cancel culture does not represent an overwhelming threat to freedom of speech. Most people who claim to be 'cancelled' have not meaningfully had their ability to broadcast their views curtailed. Most people who rail against cancel culture are concerned less with free speech in the abstract and more with their right to say specific, often offensive or even harmful things without fear of being publicly shamed or experiencing material consequences. This is because 'cancel culture' is not a progressive censoriousness that shuts down debate; instead, it is a lively discussion of contemporary social values and cultural mores that goes to the heart of changing attitudes to equality, discrimination and oppression. It represents a moral reckoning with an inequitable society that, far from attacking free speech, actually brings more people into public and political discourse, by uplifting the voices and perspectives of a wider range of people.

Free speech: a potted history

For as long as there have been arguments for free speech, there have been fights over the extent and limits of these freedoms. Early calls for freedom of speech were often rooted in Enlightenment thinking, and a rejection of either Christianity or monarchy. Free speech was the cause of radicals and progressives fighting to escape the authority of powerful controlling institutions and to speak out against orthodoxy. The revolutionary Declaration of the Rights of Man and of the Citizen, adopted by the French National Constituent Assembly in 1789, envisions freedom of speech as one of the rights that would be enjoyed by citizens of France; it remains part of the 'constitutional block' of the French Fifth Republic. The First Amendment of the US Constitution, one of the ten Amendments that make up the Bill of Rights adopted in 1791, prevents Congress from declaring a state religion or prohibiting any religious practice, or from passing laws that limit freedom of speech, freedom of the press, freedom to protest, or freedom to petition government for the redress of grievances. As well as limiting the potential power of an over-mighty government, this also continued the revolutionary principles that had underpinned the American fight against the British state in the War of Independence.

In the twentieth century, freedom of speech became one of the key distinguishing features of democracies in their clash with authoritarian regimes. In the 1941 State of the Union address, President Franklin D. Roosevelt set out the 'four freedoms' – freedom of speech, freedom of worship, freedom from want and freedom from fear – that he believed should form 'a definite basis for a kind of world attainable in our own time and generation'. Eleven months later, Japan bombed Pearl Harbor and America entered the war; the four freedoms became symbolic war aims of the US and the Allies as a whole. At the end of the war, with Allied victory, these freedoms became the rhetorical basis of the post-war settlement. The inclusion of the right to freedom of speech in the preamble to the United Nations' Universal Declaration of Human Rights (UDHR), as well as specifically in Article 19, reflected widespread global horror at the 'disregard and contempt for human rights' seen in the conflict, especially in the Holocaust and the 'barbarous acts which have outraged the conscience of mankind'.

Because of this context, freedom of speech was understood in the aftermath of the war to be a vital component of resistance to fascism. Those who sought to protect speech and expression at this time probably had in mind the figure of the jackbooted Nazi as the major threat to speakers and writers. The censorship of the Nazi state, the infamous book-burning – memorialised at Bebelplatz in Berlin by a sunken empty library with space for the 20,000 books destroyed on 10 May 1933 – understandably cast a long shadow over the post-war liberal imagination. In this context, it is not surprising that the defence of the right to speak, write and publish freely was adopted by the wider movement for tolerance, diversity and free thinking.

In reality, this conceptualisation papered over a lot of inconsistencies in the Allies' position. Censorship in wartime had been commonplace. Both Britain and the United States had suppressed political opposition to the First World War at home. In the US, the 1918 Sedition Act forbade 'disloyal, profane, scurrilous, or abusive language' about the US government, flag or military during wartime; this was repealed in 1920, but Roosevelt passed similar legislation in December 1941 with his Executive Order 8985, which allowed for the censorship of war reporting. In Britain, the 1938 Regulations for Censorship and the 1939 Emergency Powers Act allowed government to 'modify or dispose of' any publications that threatened national security or public safety; on 12 September 1939, there had been a mass government seizure of newspapers to prevent the location of the British Expeditionary Force from becoming public.[13]

At home, the British government also suppressed

the communist newspaper *Daily Worker* for more than a year, because of anxieties about the threat of communism to the war effort; this was echoed in the US Smith Act, passed in 1940, which allowed for the imprisonment of anyone who advocated for revolution against the government or who was affiliated with a revolutionary political party, and which enabled the prosecution of more than 140 American Communist Party members by 1957 under the auspices of Senator Joseph McCarthy.[14] Prior to the war, the British government had also frequently engaged in censorship to maintain its imperial power, and had controlled and suppressed information continuously throughout its imperial rule; in India, Burma and Rhodesia, for example, not just political writing but literature, films and other forms of cultural production were subject to surveillance, control and possible punishment.[15] 'Freedom of speech', as espoused by these governments, was always contingent on who was speaking and whether their views were deemed a threat to the state or to the safety of its citizens. In that sense, the right to speak and write – and to have your ideas listened to and read – has always been a privilege conferred, and potentially withdrawn, by those in power, who have been able to decide when and where and by whom freedom of speech and expression is enjoyed.

And just as free speech has always been contingent on power, there have always been many ways in which that speech might be threatened or curtailed. Broadly speaking, these can be split into penalties that are legal (the criminalisation by the government of certain types of speech, or of saying specific things), economic or social (the risk of financial penalty, such as losing one's job, or ostracisation from one's social groups or community), or cultural (a wider, generalised sense that certain topics cannot be discussed). And yet, within the international framework established by the Universal Declaration of Human Rights, freedom of speech is really and only about the first of these: the *legality* of speech. Its concern is not social or cultural, but is about the potential risk of governments prosecuting individuals or groups for saying, writing or publishing particular views, or using particular language or particular formats to do so. When the UDHR defends freedom of speech, it does so on the basis that people must be allowed to hold opinions 'without interference' from the state, and to 'seek, receive and impart information and ideas through any media and regardless of frontiers' without government interference. Likewise, the European Convention on Human Rights, which declares that 'everyone has freedom of expression', defines this as including 'the freedom to hold opinions and to receive and impart information and ideas without interference by public authority and regardless of frontiers'. In other words, neither the UDHR nor the ECHR advocates the right to speak without social and cultural consequences, only that governments should not limit people's ability to speak, listen, read or write about particular ideas or topics.

At the same time, even within these international frameworks, there has been a gradual acceptance in many countries across the second half of the twentieth century that some forms of speech are intolerable and should therefore be excluded from this legal protection, on the basis that the harm from these types of speech outweighs the social good inherent in allowing free communication. Indeed, advocates of absolute free speech – the idea that saying anything, to anyone, in any manner and at any time, should be a protected activity – are relatively rare, certainly in a formal sense. Even the United States, with its celebrated First Amendment, does not legally allow all speech in all forms;

commercial speech, for example, is not protected, meaning that misleading advertising or fraudulent material can still be prosecuted or shut down.

Many defenders of free speech do claim that it is a right that should be held above all others, or at least that it underpins other rights to such an extent that it should be prioritised, and it is certainly true that a lot of other freedoms are meaningless if people can be persecuted for talking or writing or protesting about them. This leads to arguments that we must be tolerant of speech to the maximum extent possible. And yet, free speech advocates and defenders generally accept that some very specific kinds of speech are beyond the pale. It is worth considering in what circumstances this is the case, because if it is generally agreed that some forms of speech are indeed unacceptable, then the debate about freedom of speech becomes one about where to draw the line, rather than a black and white issue of speech versus censorship.

Unacceptable speech

'Hate speech' was defined by the United Nations in 2019 as speech that 'attacks or uses pejorative or discriminatory language with reference to a person or a group on the basis of who they are'. This is a broader category of speech than the 'incitement to discrimination, hostility or violence' that is prohibited under international human rights law. In the UK, there are a variety of laws that criminalise hate speech. For example, the 1986 Public Order Act prohibits expressions of racial hatred, which are defined as 'threatening, abusive or insulting' words, written material or behaviour that 'stir up racial hatred' – either intentionally or because of the circumstances in which they are expressed – against a group because of their colour, race, nationality, national origins or ethnicity; this type of speech can be punished with a fine or up to seven years in prison. In 2006, this Act was amended to add the offence of spreading 'religious hatred'; in 2008, the Act was amended again, to criminalise hatred related to sexual orientation. These laws have been controversial, particularly those regarding religious hatred: in 2013, campaigners successfully convinced the government to remove a reference that forbade 'insulting' speech about religion, on the grounds that this constituted censorship, rather than the prevention of actual harm. But the principle behind laws prohibiting hate speech – that some speech is not worthy of protection and should not be allowed to be broadcast in public or directed against specific individuals – is very widely accepted, and has been for some time. For example, the 1969 International Convention on the Elimination of All Forms of Racial Discrimination, a United Nations Convention adopted by 188 parties, required its signatories to criminalise both hate speech and membership of racist organisations, thus theoretically infringing on both freedom of speech and freedom of association (although many signatories – including the UK, the USA, France, Ireland and Japan – have registered reservations rejecting this requirement or agreeing to implement it only partially or in particular circumstances).

In the United States, the First Amendment prevents laws against hate speech, but there are other means of prosecuting it. Speech inciting hatred against individuals and groups can be stopped if it takes the form of a specific threat of violence ('true threats' or 'fighting words') or incites imminent criminal activity; these fall into the small number of categories of speech that are not protected by the First Amendment, alongside fraudulent speech, obscenity, defamation and child pornography. Even in the US, then, where freedom of speech has exceptional protections in the Constitution, there are in fact both practical and legal limitations on what can be said.

There are other examples of laws prohibiting speech which many people agree are necessary or morally valuable. Germany, for example, prohibits Holocaust denial, in legislation that forbids the incitement of hatred against groups based on religious, national or ethnic origin, as well as prohibiting speech that praises, downplays or denies acts committed by the Nazi government, or that glorifies or justifies Nazi rule. Similarly, Austrian legislation passed in 1947 specifically bans the Nazi Party and includes within it provisions against Nazi propaganda including the prohibition of Holocaust denial. Several other countries have also seen fit to criminalise writing or speech that denies the reality or facts of the Holocaust, or to prohibit genocide denial more widely: these include seventeen European countries, among them France (1990), Belgium (1995), Luxembourg (1997), the Czech Republic (2001) and Bulgaria (2011), plus Israel (1986) and Russia (2014). In Bosnia-Herzegovina, the international authorities in the Office of the High Representative outlawed genocide denial and the glorification of war criminals in 2021 to counter the rising trend of denialism of the scope of the 1995 Srebrenica massacre.

The European Union attempted to pass an EU-wide prohibition of Holocaust denial but was prevented by the United Kingdom (then a member state) and Sweden, Denmark and Norway, specifically because these governments believed that the law would clash with freedom of speech. Eventually, the EU agreed a measure that allowed member states to opt in to a three-year jail sentence for any speech 'denying or grossly trivialising crimes of genocide, crimes against humanity and war crimes'; the UK did not choose to adopt this before withdrawing from the organisation, and Holocaust denial remains legal in British law.

Even so, the UK was host to one of the most notorious legal cases in relation to Holocaust denial. David Irving sued Deborah Lipstadt and her publisher, Penguin Books, for defamation when she characterised him as 'one of the most dangerous spokespersons for Holocaust denial' in her book *Denying the Holocaust* (1993) and claimed that he had manipulated historical evidence to suit his argument. Lipstadt's lawyers, calling on expert witnesses such as the historian Richard Evans, were forced to build a case that Irving had deliberately sought to lie about the Holocaust in his body of work; Evans, in his book *Telling Lies About Hitler*, argued that the trial 'demonstrated triumphantly the ability of historical scholarship to reach reasoned conclusions about the Nazi extermination of the Jews on the basis of a careful examination of the written evidence'.[16] It is worth pointing out that neither Evans nor Lipstadt supports the existence of laws criminalising the denial of the Holocaust; in fact, in this scenario, it was Irving who was trying – and who ultimately failed – to curtail Lipstadt's speech, in his use of defamation laws against her.

The fact that Irving could bring a defamation case against Lipstadt demonstrates that Holocaust denial might be legal in the United Kingdom but it is not considered morally acceptable or academically legitimate. There is, in fact, a general understanding that Holocaust denial is unacceptable speech that must be countered – 'discredited', in Evans' words[17] – and prevented from being disseminated. But as we have noted, in other countries, Holocaust denial is not countered simply with moral censure but with criminal proceedings, and Irving himself was sentenced to three years in prison in early 2006 by a court in Vienna after he was apprehended on a warrant that had been issued for his arrest in 1989; he was released from prison in December 2006 and again banned from entering Austria.[18] The year before, the neo-Nazi publisher Ernst Zündel had been extradited from Canada to Germany and sentenced to five years' imprisonment for Holocaust denial, despite his supporters' claims that he was merely an advocate for free speech.[19] It is not only Germany and Austria that have sought to imprison people for denying the Holocaust; in Australia, the activist Fredrick Töben was imprisoned for three months in 2009 for publishing denialist material on the website of the Adelaide Institute, a neo-Nazi organisation that he ran.[20]

What this shows is that even in countries that pride themselves on being bastions of free speech, certain categories of speech are considered beyond the pale, both morally and legally. This is because we recognise that public speech has *consequences* and these flow from its *contents*. On this basis, countries have implemented laws that clearly limit their citizens' rights to absolute freedom of speech in service of other rights – such as the right of citizens to live without fear of racial abuse – or higher principles, including that of historical truth. Defamation laws are also in place to deter the libel or slander of individuals; laws around commercial speech prevent false advertising and fraudulent activity. And governments such as those of the USA and UK have often attempted to control speech in order to suppress opposition to their domestic, foreign and imperial policies. There is no clear precedent for uncontrolled speech in history – and that's before you get to the question of who historically has had the ability and resources to make themselves heard.

But today's debate about freedom of speech is not, generally, about what is legally permissible or allowed by the state. It is about what is culturally acceptable, and allowed by societies. The risk that is imagined in these debates is not usually curtailment of speech by state and law, but the suppression of speech by the economic and social consequences of a hostile audience: censure, not censorship. Fundamentally, this is a debate about the legitimacy of different political, social or moral positions, not about the right to speak in and of itself. And the panic over 'cancellation' is not really about whether people are allowed to speak, but about whether they can avoid the consequences of what they have said.

Don't cancel me

Around the end of the Second World War, in a preface to his satirical novel *Animal Farm* (1945), the author George Orwell expressed anxiety about this different kind of 'threat' to free speech. (The preface was not published with the novel and did not appear publicly until it was unearthed by his biographer and printed in the *Times Literary Supplement* in 1972.) Orwell was intimately familiar with government information control during the war, having worked for the BBC spreading Ministry of Information material while his wife worked in its censorship division. In his preface, he declared that government actions in the conflict had been largely acceptable: 'during this war official censorship has not been particularly irksome . . . on the whole the Government has behaved well and has been surprisingly tolerant of minority opinions.'[21]

Instead, Orwell had another target in his sights. He had initially attempted to publish *Animal Farm* with four publishers, all of whom had rejected it.

He was particularly angry at one of them, Jonathan Cape, who had decided that the book's criticism of the Soviet Union, allies of the British since 1941, 'might be regarded as something which it was highly ill-advised to publish at the present time'. Jonathan Cape decided to withdraw support from the book after a discussion with the Ministry of Information, and Orwell was informed of this explicitly; even if there was no formal censorship involved here, government intervention had clearly played some role in Cape's decision. But in Orwell's view, if the government had not officially banned his book, then Cape's rejection of it was actually worse: an act of self-censorship which was indicative of what he saw as the 'intellectual cowardice' of British cultural elites. In his essay he railed against the 'prevailing orthodoxy' of the 'literary and scientific intelligentsia', which prevented controversial ideas from being published without any need for formal government intervention: 'If publishers and editors exert themselves to keep certain topics out of print, it is not because they are frightened of prosecution but because they are frightened of public opinion.'[22]

Orwell's essay is partly a rant about the negative reviews that he expected to receive for *Animal*

Farm – reviews that he believed would be politically motivated – and partly an attack on the liberal groupthink that had designated attacks on the Soviet Union as simply 'not done'. Above all – and despite the glaring evidence that the government did play a key role – Orwell blamed fear of public opinion for his book's 'suppression'. In this way, he rather perfectly foreshadowed today's panic about progressive censoriousness, cancel culture, and those cultural gatekeepers who bow to it – as well as one of its key ironies. Far from being suppressed, *Animal Farm* sold half a million copies in its first year of publication and is today one of the most read books in the English language.

Similarly to Orwell's concerns, the recent panic about cancel culture derives from the fear that certain political or cultural views have been deemed unacceptable by a hyper-sensitive, self-righteous group that has taken it upon itself to police what people can say, write or even think: the 'woke mob'. Fox News seems to have embraced this term on its website and TV coverage from late 2020 or early 2021; a typical piece in July 2021 was entitled 'The woke mob is everywhere: Here's where it came from and how one critic believes it can be stopped'.[23] In Britain, Piers Morgan was using the term in a column in the *Mail on Sunday* as early as 2019: 'the ghastly "CANCEL EVERYONE!" woke mob have been temporarily put back in their virtue-signalling little box.'[24] By 2022, the *New Yorker* could run a humour piece entitled 'Ways the Woke Mob Has Affected Me Personally', including 'woke baristas' still playing, but *not being into*, 'old-white-guy' music in local coffee shops.[25]

This language evokes 'mob rule', a persistent fear in British political history, the idea of the unruly mob dating back to the Glorious Revolution of 1688 and concerns about the *mobile vulgus*, the 'excitable crowd' that seemed always to be at the gate of the frightened establishment.[26] Similarly, the spectre of the woke mob invokes the fear that anybody can be cancelled for their views or ideas at any time. In reality, though, the bogeyman of cancellation is almost entirely invoked by conservatives against their detractors. As Amia Srinivasan has pointed out, the term 'cancelled' has its own 'substantively political' agenda, which connects it implicitly to censure from the left, or from a progressive perspective. 'It would sound plain weird to say that someone has been "cancelled" by the right', Srinivasan argues, because 'when the right does it, it's an exercise of free speech'.[27] In this sense, 'to cancel' is an irregular verb, governed by where you stand on the political spectrum: *the conservative* has been cancelled by oversensitive progressive bullies, whereas *the progressive* has been 'owned' and their speech discredited in the marketplace of ideas.

The idea of a new 'progressive censoriousness' is attractive to conservatives for two reasons. First, it positions them as a brave resistance to the woke mob, cancelled for daring to speak truth to power (rather than, say, for being racist or homophobic). Second, by casting progressives in the role of the censor, the term seeks to undermine their claim to the moral high ground. Isn't it *ironic*, conservatives seem to say, that these self-proclaimed progressives all eventually become totalitarians? From this point of view, all laws aimed at protecting the vulnerable – whether from hate speech or cigarette smoke – are invariably seen as the overreach of a 'nanny state' that is patronising at best and dangerous at worst. To give an example: the right-wing British think tank, the Institute for Economic Affairs, has produced material on threats to freedom of speech, arguing that young people are being 'socialised into a censoriousness . . . reminiscent of totalitarian regimes', but also that comedians are being 'inhibited' by 'political correctness' and that advertising regulation is 'a form of social engineering'; the IEA's 'Head of Lifestyle Economics', Christopher Snowden, also compiles a 'Nanny State Index', a system that ranks different nations based on consumer freedoms in the markets of alcohol, nicotine, and food and soft drink.[28]

The ideological connection between threats to free speech and the spectre of the nanny state serves to bolster both positions as cornerstones of conservative thinking, and activists in both arenas often depict themselves as brave and pioneering defenders against government overreach and in support of freedom. In this way, for example, the conservative website UnHerd, funded by Paul Marshall (a hedge-fund millionaire who donated significant sums to the Brexit campaign and the Conservative Party), proclaims itself to be 'challenging the herd' when it publishes writers such as Douglas Murray, a prolific critic of immigration, Islam and 'identity politics'. The idea that somebody runs the risk of 'cancellation' can be used as a way to suggest that the speaker's ideas are not only correct, but also that they are dangerously – excitingly – radical; for which reason, the person is worth listening to, and taking seriously. Potential cancellation becomes, in other words, a badge of honour.

In the field of British imperial history – the academic field in which I teach and publish – there has been a consistent attempt by a group of scholars to depict themselves as the victims of woke cancellation. These conservative academics object to the direction of historical research into this topic and are concerned that a newer generation of historians are 'rewriting' the historical narrative to fit their ideological agenda. In 2023, this academic conflict reached a wider audience when the *Guardian* ran an exploration by Samira Shackle into the controversy around historical research at Gonville and Caius College, Cambridge. In the wake of the Black Lives Matter movement and a reckoning with British imperial history, researcher Nico Bell-Romero had been commissioned to write a report exploring the connections between the university and the slave trade. But when he and his colleague Bronwen Everill came to circulate the report internally, their work was dismissed as a 'fad' by emeritus academics at Caius College who claimed the researchers had 'an agenda' in developing their research and tried – but failed – to prevent the publication of the report.[29]

In the case of Gonville and Caius College, it was clearly progressives, rather than conservatives, who saw their right to freedom of speech attacked. And yet the narrative has taken hold, both in Britain and the US, that it is right-wing academics who run the risk of being 'cancelled' by a conformist, progressive, academic establishment. This narrative has been brewing for some time. In 2017, the political scientist Bruce Gilley wrote a piece for *Third World Quarterly*, titled 'The Case for Colonialism', in which he argued that widespread criticism of colonialism was the result of a new intellectual orthodoxy that refused to see the evidence that European empires had been both 'objectively' 'beneficial' and 'subjectively' 'legitimate' entities.[30] This piece was eventually pulled from the journal's website following the resignation of fifteen members of its editorial board, although the reason given for its removal was not the widespread protest with which it had been received but the 'serious and credible' threats of violence made against the editor.[31] But its removal was enough to convince many people that the field of imperial history was caught in a chokehold of normative wokeness.

Perhaps the loudest voice here was that of Nigel Biggar, a theology professor at the University of

Oxford, who wrote an impassioned piece for *The Times* that November – 'Don't Feel Guilty About Our Colonial History' – in which he decried the 'perfect storm of protest' that had greeted Gilley's work and attacked the idea 'that our imperial past was one long, unbroken litany of oppression, exploitation and self-deception'.[32] Much of the critique of Gilley had been focused on his work's academic limitations which meant, arguably, that it should never have been published; indeed, the piece had been rejected by peer reviewers and so was published in the 'Viewpoints' section of the journal.[33] But Biggar did not engage with the serious academic criticisms of Gilley's work, which he instead characterised as a 'fury of indignation'. Nor in fact did he argue explicitly that Gilley's free speech had been infringed or that he had been 'cancelled' – although he did label his work 'courageous', implying that publishing entailed some risk. He was more focused on defending the ideas that Gilley had presented. But this was merely the first salvo of what would become a running battle.

Nigel Biggar is not an academic historian, but his commitment (against the grain of much contemporary historical scholarship) to a triumphalist narrative of imperial history was so strong that he had recently launched a research project to support it. 'Ethics and Empire' was funded through the McDonald Centre for Theology, Ethics and Public Life, of which Biggar was the founder. The project aimed to explore the ethical history of imperialism and develop lessons from imperial history to be applied to the modern world. News of this project had been met with concern from people at his own institution and more widely. The student group Common Ground criticised the 'inaccuracy' and 'lack of rigour' in Biggar's article supporting Gilley, raised questions about the research's funding, asked whether faculty and students of colour had been consulted in its design, and argued that Biggar was an 'inauspicious and inappropriate leader' for the work.[34] Fifty-eight Oxford academics whose research focused on empire also registered their concern. In an open letter, the historians were careful to set out that Biggar 'has every right to hold and to express whatever views he chooses or finds compelling', before stating their professional critique of the project: that the existence of a new historical orthodoxy was 'nonsense', and that he was asking 'the wrong questions, using the wrong terms, and for the wrong purposes'. They also pointed out that the entire project would, unusually for academia, be run through 'closed, invitation-only seminars' seemingly designed to shield the research from critical eyes.[35]

None of this was an assault on Biggar's free speech, but an engagement – albeit a critical one – with the premise of his research and academic perspective. But this was not how it was received. A spokesperson for the University of Oxford gave a statement to the press which began: 'We absolutely support academic freedom of speech', and defended Biggar as 'an internationally recognised authority'.[36] Biggar described the letter by his fellow academics as a 'virtual mobbing', and said he had become a 'pariah' in his institution.[37] At Cheltenham Literary Festival the following summer, Biggar was invited to speak about his work, and The Times' coverage of his talk argued that his experiences demonstrated 'a worrying slide towards Stalinism on campuses'.[38] The fact that Biggar had been invited to speak at Cheltenham, but that none of his critics had been granted the same platform, did not seem to register as being in any way at odds with the notion of Biggar's 'cancellation'.

Since the launch of the Ethics and Empire project, Biggar has repeatedly claimed that there is a cohort of academics who are being silenced on colonial history because they are afraid to speak out in support of 'unfashionable causes' for fear of being 'mobbed'.[39] It is hard if not impossible to substantiate Biggar's claim because of the inherent challenge of assessing how many people secretly agree with something. During the immediate backlash to the publication of his essay, Bruce Gilley had himself argued that it should be taken down from the *Third World Quarterly* website. Later, in a piece published by the conservative magazine *Standpoint*, entitled 'How the Hate Mob Tried to Silence Me', Gilley argued that the calls to remove his essay were 'Maoist', and that academics had sought 'to punish dissenting voices' which dared to praise colonialism 'with *Pravda*-like ferocity'. He also blamed the tone of the debate for forcing him into 'self-censorship' with his own apology. It is striking that the 'death threats' by 'Indian anti-colonial fanatics' against the editorial staff that led to his essay being taken down – which do seem like a fairly clear-cut example of free speech being threatened – appear far less concerning to Gilley than the 'hundreds of tenured professors' who spoke out against the content of his piece: the woke mob was presented as a far greater threat to his freedom of speech than the actual threats of violence which led to his speech being censored.[40]

Biggar is likewise regularly described by the right-wing press as having been 'cancelled' or 'ostra-cised'.[41] In January 2023, it was reported in *The Times* that his publisher Bloomsbury had decided to delay indefinitely publication of his book *Colonialism: A Moral Reckoning* as 'conditions are not currently favourable', and had offered to pay Biggar the balance of his advance and release him from his contract if he wanted to publish sooner; the author had responded with anger at what he saw as 'the expansion of authoritarianism and the shrinking of moral and political diversity'.[42] A few days later, Biggar wrote a long piece for *MailOnline* claiming that his manuscript had been 'cancelled' because of political pressure: 'Bloomsbury would rather pay me off than publish', he argued in a piece entitled: 'The publishing industry is killing free speech and spreading lies – by cancelling authors like me'.[43] But the book had already found a new publisher, William Collins, an imprint of Rupert Murdoch-owned HarperCollins, and had been published in the week that the *MailOnline* piece appeared. Thanks at least in part to the storm of coverage his book's cancelling received, it became an instant *Sunday Times* bestseller.

All told, Biggar's cancellation seems to have brought him significant financial and professional reward. Not only was he paid twice for his book, it probably received far more coverage and commercial success than it would have otherwise. In 2021, he was made a Commander of the British Empire; he told *The Times* that this was 'because of my engagement with the issue of free speech and academic freedom in universities', which 'involves being able to speak freely and do research on things colonial and the British Empire in a manner that may conclude that the British Empire and colonialism were not all bad'.[44] Cancellation can have its benefits, it seems.

Not only that, the large number of editorials that Biggar has been able to place across the British press, his numerous speaking engagements and the success of his book all point to the fact that his 'cancellation' has had the effect of elevating and amplifying his freedom of speech rather than silencing him. That's not to say that cancellation always has such beneficial effects. But it would be sensible to be cautious whenever claims of cancellation are being made, loudly and prominently, in the most established and visible platforms the media has to offer, by the very people who are claiming their voice has been stifled.

New powers

This is also not to say that there have been no casualties to cancelling or that this process is always professionally beneficial (or morally justified). Social media has enabled a knee-jerk response to speech which can lead to people being unfairly attacked and ostracised, or harassed, shamed or even fired or forced to resign. It should be acknowledged, however, that much of the threat to 'ordinary' people's jobs in these moments comes not from the 'woke mob' itself but from a concern with reputation management that means employers increasingly police their employees' speech and actions in their personal life as well as at work. This can hardly be typified as progressive censoriousness, not least because people are censured at work for espousing support for 'progressive' causes as often as for conservative ones; for example, the police detective in Massachusetts who was fired for posting a picture of her niece at a Black Lives Matter protest, or the doctor in Birmingham who was suspended from practising for five months after she was arrested at a Just Stop Oil demonstration.[45] As for internet harassment – which can extend to deeply unpleasant behaviours such as doxing and death threats – this clearly can limit speech and people's ability to say what they believe without censure. Again, though, it should be acknowledged that it is overwhelmingly people perceived to be on the 'woke' end of the spectrum who experience the worst of this, with women of colour being the most likely to face abuse online. The think tank Chatham House has highlighted, for example, the experiences of Diane Abbott and Nadia Whittome, both Labour MPs who as women of colour receive an astonishing amount of harassment and abuse online.[46]

Ultimately, the power of the 'woke mob' derives not from the ability to imprison or silence forcibly – it is not, truly, censorship in that regard – but from its ability to heckle, to protest and to mobilise via social media. This use of public 'calling out' *may* then pressurise large institutions into removing invitations to speak, or forcing people from their jobs, but in reality this is fairly uncommon. Most of the time, the 'woke mob' wakens to express annoyance, hurt or anger at the ideas being presented by somebody

who will face very few, if any, tangible consequences; these people may be briefly shamed, but
as seen in the frequent coverage of these moments
in the media – in which the cancelled are usually
given a platform from which to justify their position
and often to restate the views that led to their 'cancellation' in the first place – they are almost never
actually silenced in any meaningful way. In fact, in
some fields, such as writing opinion columns, a good
cancellation scandal is probably advantageous for
driving traffic to the publication website and developing a strong brand for the writer.

Often, therefore, if we were to label these
supposed cancellations as what they actually are –
the calling out of ideas – then such activity starts
to look less like an attack on freedom of speech
and much more like an instrument, sometimes
blunt, sometimes clumsy, that is being used in the
renegotiation of the moral boundaries of public
discourse. In this light, the fervour over 'cancellation' is in reality a reckoning with social mores
and cultural norms that have developed and shifted
over time; at times very quickly, in reaction to a
particular moment or event, and other times more
subtly, over the course of a lifetime or longer. It is
natural for these shifts to feel uncomfortable for

people who find that things they used to say are no longer acceptable, but this should not be allowed to obscure the fact that many other people now feel relief that these attitudes are being challenged. Whose rights are more important? For example: the right of a person to use racial slurs in public (even if, perhaps, those slurs used to be 'acceptable'), or the right of people of colour to exist in the public sphere without facing abuse? Of course, not all cases are this clear-cut, and moments of 'cancellation' where the speech in question is not universally accepted as offensive are more difficult to balance. But at its heart, this is about a transference of power in public discourse: who gets to feel comfortable, who is made to feel discomfort, and what effect this has. It is not about censorship.

It is also important to recognise that when people do turn to 'cancellation' as a tactic, it is often because they lack other means of bringing about change in society. When groups of people mobilise to call out a celebrity or a politician for something they have said, the 'woke mob' might appear to be a very real and dangerous foe. But the power dynamic here is largely unchanged from that seen in the past: those with power enjoy a high-profile public platform, and those who are expected to listen can do little more than heckle in response; what has changed is that social media enables these responses to be preserved and amplified, in a way that encourages others to add their voice. It is their relative powerlessness that makes progressives appear sensitive and censorious: calling out the things people say and write that betray racist, misogynist or homophobic ways of thinking is one of the few concrete things they can do to address the racism, misogyny and homophobia that pervade society, but which they have no direct means of changing. A focus on language is not a meaningless or trivial diversion: it is a stepping stone to systemic change that might often seem out of reach in the moment.

Much of the concern about cancel culture is the concern of powerful people that they might face opprobrium for their views – which could lead to them losing their position of power, but which might simply come as a shock when they are unused to being held to account in any way. It is no coincidence that this concern was less pressing before social media, when those in positions of political and cultural power – politicians, academics, journalists – were more insulated from criticism and more able to control the terms of debates. When the acceptable boundaries of discourse, language and ideologies were set by the establishment – often in ways that undermined, insulted or discriminated against minority groups – those in power could more comfortably express views that did the same. Now that there is a wider movement towards inclusive language and against discrimination, and now that minoritised and vulnerable groups can make their own voices heard more effectively, the fact that those in power feel less secure in expressing themselves and are more worried about the consequences they might face is, surely, a good thing.

Campus culture, cancel culture

Many of those who express concerns about free speech being under threat are worried understandably for particular individuals – including, usually, themselves. And yet it would be unfair to characterise this panic as driven only by self-interest. Many also express anxiety that audiences and society more broadly are suffering from the stifling effect of cancel culture, which via fear-induced self-censorship deprives us of important opportunities to engage with difficult ideas. For a while in British politics it became common, for example, to hear the complaint that people simply 'could not talk about immigration' without being labelled reactionary bigots. In a speech to Conservative MPs and candidates in 2005, then leader of the party Michael Howard bemoaned the fact that 'for too long, people have felt unable to talk about their proper and legitimate concerns' and stated that it was 'not racist to talk about immigration'; in a speech in 2021, Priti Patel, then Home Secretary, echoed this sentiment, saying that, for too long, 'too many were happy to assert that even raising the topic of immigration was racist'.[47] In the arts, meanwhile, there's a persistent argument that audiences are newly unwilling to be challenged. In 2024, for example, actors including Ralph Fiennes and Matt Smith spoke about the use of 'trigger warnings' in theatre; Fiennes argued that theatre has the prerogative to 'shock and disturb' audiences, while Smith asked: 'Isn't art meant to be dangerous?'[48]

Of course, people have always been able to express hostility to immigration in British politics; when Enoch Powell made his 'Rivers of Blood' speech in 1968 he was sacked from the front bench and attacked in much of the mainstream press, but he also experienced a huge outpouring of public support and sustained his political career for some time. Likewise, it is worth remembering that in Britain all theatre was subject to the censorship of the Lord Chamberlain until 1968: it may well be the case that the legitimate boundaries of drama and performance in this country are shifting, but given that within living memory the state could criminally prosecute theatres for staging plays it had not approved, a little perspective might be warranted here.

Even if it is true that audiences, as well as speakers, do indeed lose out in a world where the acceptable boundaries of debate are being narrowed and policed by a culture of censoriousness, it is equally true that social mores are always in need of reappraisal, and that the acceptable terms of debate and discussion *must* therefore adapt and shift across time. Perhaps the most pertinent question is whether we have entered a new era of *excessively* restrictive censoriousness, or if we are simply witnessing a familiar – and historically speaking, relatively moderate – adjustment of what is considered appropriate and acceptable. To answer this question, it is helpful to think about one group often cited as particularly at risk in the free speech wars, not only because of what they might say but because of what they might not be allowed to hear: university students.

The idea of university as a space in which people should expect to be exposed to different arguments and perspectives is pervasive. In fact, the argument goes, a full and rounded education necessarily involves being exposed to challenging ideas. By this logic, as with that of theatre and the arts, the bounds of what is acceptable speech on university campus should be as wide as possible, and possibly wider than in most other areas of public life. And yet, we are often told that it is university students who are particularly engaged in shutting down speech that they don't like on the basis that they don't feel 'comfortable' or 'safe' around certain dissenting opinions. The former chair of the Office for Students, the British university regulatory body, argued that students do not need to be 'protected from ideas that . . . may make them feel uncomfortable', and that university should instead be a place where 'unpopular ideas are debated rather than suppressed'; in fact, he has argued, 'feeling uncomfortable is an essential ingredient of learning'.[49]

The proportion of young people going in to higher education has risen dramatically in both the UK and the USA since the Second World War, but they still represent a minority of society as a whole. Nonetheless, students loom especially large in the popular imagination because they are thought to express and embody the awakening political voice of a new generation, a group of people who still suffer from the dangerous idealism of youth while wielding the very real power of the vote. Typically they are in their teens and early twenties, and so concerns about their politics and positions are entangled with broader generational concerns – in today's case about the so-called 'snowflake' generation, Gen Z, who are thought to be especially brittle and predominantly 'woke'. (In comparison, conservative students (and academics) are assumed to be an ostracised minority on most campuses, cowed into silence for having views that are unacceptable to censorious progressives.[50]) In other words, panics about 'campus cancel culture' ought to be understood as part of a generalised generational panic about the supposed intolerance of youth, something that has always been an anxiety among older generations about their younger counterparts.

By the same token, today's students are really no different from those of a previous generation, inasmuch as they are reacting against and criticising their forebears. After all, the students of the 1960s and 1970s were famously unshy about making their views known when it came to who should be given airtime to speak on campus, forcefully disrupting various speakers' visits with protests, pickets and heckling. 1968 was a particularly fractious year in the UK. In February, University of Sussex students threw red paint over a visiting press officer from the United States Embassy as part of a protest against the Vietnam War. In April, Patrick Gordon Walker, Secretary of State for Education and Science, visited the University of Manchester to address a regional planning seminar on polytechnics, but was prevented from speaking by students who shouted 'First things first, talk about grants!' and blocked his exit when he tried to leave. That June, student demonstrators at the University of Bradford prevented Duncan Sandys, the Conservative MP for Streatham, from addressing a meeting of the student Conservative association; when Sandys attempted to move his speech outside 'with the help of a loud hailer', he was still interrupted by 'heckling and shouts of "Sandys go home" and "racialist".[51] In fact, students often went well beyond what might be considered legitimate protest. When the Home Secretary Jim Callaghan visited Nuffield College, Oxford after his government had passed the controversial 1968 Immigration Act, students threatened to throw him in the college pond; when Patrick Wall

MP, a Conservative associated with the far-right Monday Club, spoke at the University of Leeds in the same year, he was spat on by student protesters and his wife was kicked to the ground.[52] In the US in the same period, protests around the Vietnam War involved picketing and heckling of speakers, as well as demands for no-platforming. Across the country, students objected to campus recruitment talks by Dow Chemicals Company as the principal supplier of napalm to the US Defense Department; at the University of Pennsylvania, protesters organised a sit-in to interrupt a recruitment event and eventually the Dow representative was forced off campus, a scenario that played out across many other universities.[53] University campuses in Britain and America were volatile spaces in the 1960s, 1970s and beyond.

Indeed, the leftist radicalism of this earlier generation is often cited as one of the root causes of today's problems. From the end of the twentieth century to the present day there has been a constant thread of commentary focusing on the university campus (or 'college campus' in the US) as a fundamentally illiberal space, one governed by the iron fist of progressives who wish to control how people speak and think about political and cultural issues. There has been a range of books published on this topic, from Dinesh D'Souza's *Illiberal Education: The Politics of Race and Sex on Campus* (1991) to Jonathan Haidt and Greg Lukianoff's *The Coddling of the American Mind* (2018), which make roughly the same argument: higher education has been captured by progressive elites who seek to impose their values on everyone else, and in doing so have created a culture of intolerance on campus where – the ironic twist in this tale! – it is the conservatives who find themselves outnumbered and silenced. According to this argument, the radical and intolerant progressives of a previous student generation have only themselves to blame for the hypersensitive intolerance of today's students, which is now coming back to bite them. And lurking just beneath the surface is a thinly veiled subtext: that today's young people do not know how to have fun, that they are less likely to let their hair down, that they are po-faced and stuck up.

At the heart of these arguments is a fundamentally patronising assumption that young people today have not arrived at their views of their own volition; they are assumed to be the unwitting products (or victims) of circumstance, rather than politically independent thinkers whose actions are based on a distinct rationale that deserves to be addressed, and who are rooted in a longstanding tradition. No-platforming – refusing to allow a speaker or an organisation a platform from which to share their views – has long been a critical tool in British student politics, particularly in the fight against the far right. It was common in the 1970s for students to disrupt speakers and events associated with the National Front, after the National Union of Students adopted a no-platform policy that encouraged students to 'prevent any member of these organisations or individuals known to espouse similar views from speaking in colleges by whatever means necessary'.

At the time, the *Guardian* was concerned that this policy was anti-democratic, a 'classic pattern of fascism'.[54] And the most common critiques of no-platforming are, first, that it involves bowing to intimidation and ceding power to those who are loudest and most threatening, and second, that silencing a person does nothing to defeat their ideas and may even have the opposite effect. Even if these arguments were true, however, are there really no circumstances in which it is legitimate to rescind someone's invitation to speak publicly, or to refuse to give them that opportunity in the first place? Is every institution compelled to invite every speaker to present their ideas, and is every invitation a binding agreement that cannot ever be reconsidered or torn up?

One problem with the critique of no-platforming is that it effectively posits an ideal world in which all speakers have an equal opportunity to speak. Cancelling an invitation is regarded as an act of intolerance because it denies a person their right to speak and be heard. But what about those people who don't even have the opportunity to be denied that right, because they were never invited in the first place? The rights of those would-be speakers who are not well connected or politically palatable enough to be invited to speak at eminent, newsworthy institutions are rarely explored in this analysis.

These concerns about (no-)platforming tend to be inconsistently applied across different political persuasions. The indignation is almost always about conservative speakers – even those espousing far-right views – being no-platformed by liberal or left-wing institutions or audiences. There is very little outcry, on the other hand, that conservative spaces rarely choose to hear from speakers on the radical left; the idea that a hedge fund might choose to invite a speaker from the Occupy movement, for example, is laughable. The UK Ministry of Defence, Home Office and Department of Education have all recently cancelled, or attempted to cancel, talks from experts when it was found that those people had been critical of government policy.[55] There is an assumption that platforming a range of speakers is crucial for the creation of a wider culture of openness, democracy and civility in debate – the idea that we should all be willing to listen to and learn from people across the political spectrum. And yet, somehow, it is always one side of the argument which is expected to be open to the other, and never the other way around.

Meanwhile, some of the most high-profile instances of outcry against no-platforming are tendentious to the point of absurdity. In 2020, for example, the former Conservative Home Secretary Amber Rudd was invited to speak at the University of Oxford by the UNWomen Oxford student society to mark International Women's Day, but was then disinvited after disagreement among the hosts. The advertised talk had already attracted criticism because Rudd had been forced to resign as Home Secretary two years earlier in connection with the Windrush scandal that had seen at least eighty-three people wrongfully deported from the

UK. The student society had initially attempted to defuse the situation with the promise that they would have 'an honest and frank conversation about how her policies have impacted women of all races, religions, classes etcetera'.[56] Thirty minutes before the event was due to start, however, the society announced on Facebook that they had cancelled the talk after the organising committee had voted in favour of disinviting the MP. In the outcry that followed, figures from across the political spectrum bemoaned the illiberalism of the students who had rescinded Rudd's invitation to speak, and the incivility with which they had done so. And yet, could anyone really argue that the ex-Home Secretary of the United Kingdom had been 'cancelled' or silenced, or that her freedom of speech had been curtailed because of this act of de-platforming? Some inevitably argued that the principles of free speech were at stake – the University of Oxford itself stated that it 'strongly disapprove[d]' of the decision to disinvite Rudd as an institution that was 'committed to freedom of speech and oppose[d] no-platforming', while many Conservative politicians, as well as Rudd herself, expressed their dismay that she had been 'no-platformed'.[57] But in reality, the objections seemed to stem more from the idea that, in light of Rudd's status, the society's revocation had been 'rude'.[58] Leaving aside the fact that suffering the rudeness of others is in a politician's job description (witness Prime Minister's Questions), rudeness itself does not constitute an infringement of rights; the rudeness of somebody's opposition to your speech has no bearing on whether their opposition is legitimate. And whether Amber Rudd has the right to speak at all, or whether she has the right to speak to a specific student society at the University of Oxford after they have decided to rescind their invitation to her, are two different questions.

The fact of Amber Rudd's political identity no doubt exacerbated the whole furore, but it came on the back of a rising tide of conservative – and Conservative – concern about 'free speech' on campus, which was often conflated with the right of right-wing speakers to express their views without protest or criticism. On 1 January 2018 – two years before Rudd's invitation was revoked – the Conservative government had created the new Office for Students through the amalgamation of two bodies, the state-run Higher Education Funding Council for England and the independent Office for Fair Access, which together managed university funding and regulation. The newly minted OfS was given an extended remit to focus specifically on student experience – and the facet of experience with which it was and is most concerned is freedom of speech, as evidenced by its initial appointment to its governing board of the right-wing commentator and head of the Free Speech Union, Toby Young. (Young was forced to resign almost immediately after his appointment when a series of social media posts surfaced which showed he had, among other things, made derogatory remarks about working-class undergraduates, disability access policies, and the bodies of female politicians.[59]) When Amber Rudd was de-platformed, Gavin Williamson, then Education Secretary, responded in the moment by stating that 'if universities are not prepared to defend free speech, the government will'.[60] The following summer the Conservative government introduced the Higher Education (Freedom of Speech) Bill, which it heralded as 'a huge step forward in protecting freedom of speech and academic freedom on campuses'.[61] The bill required universities, colleges and student unions to take steps to protect freedom of speech on campus, allowed students, staff and visiting speakers to take claims to court if they felt that their speech had been curtailed, and created a position of a 'free speech tsar' for universities, a role that was subsequently filled by the Cambridge philosopher Arif Ahmed.

The bill was extremely controversial in its passage to law, not least because the universities minister, Michelle Donelan, seemed unclear as to whether the legislation could be used to support speakers who wanted to engage in Holocaust denial.[62] It received sustained criticism from groups including Index on Censorship, English PEN and Article 19, who claimed that the bill would actually 'have the inverse effect of further limiting what is deemed "acceptable" speech on campus and introducing a chilling effect both on the content of what is taught and the scope of academic research exploration'.[63] But those who had positioned themselves against 'cancel culture' on campus celebrated the bill's passing: Eric Kaufmann, the conservative academic, described it as 'a huge step towards saving the soul of university education'.[64]

As Amia Srinivasan has pointed out, a major problem with this bill, and with critiques of no-platforming in general, is the conflation of freedom of speech with 'academic freedom' (or indeed other kinds of freedom), for the latter may very well involve the withholding or withdrawing of a platform from someone whose ideas we believe to be wrong or irresponsible or dangerous. In her example, if a climate change denier wanted to speak at Oxford University, 'it is presumably within the rights of Oxford's geography dons – world experts in ecological change and crisis – to deny him a platform or a job'.[65] Another limitation of the bill, perhaps more foundational, is that it fails to understand what makes public speech so powerful. It is a form of action that itself can have direct and profound consequences, including harmful ones, and those who resort to no-platforming or de-platforming are acting almost always from a position of relative powerlessness. Once we recognise this it becomes much clearer why some acts of silencing and no-platforming might be justifiable or even necessary.

Part of the problem with claims that invited speakers are being 'silenced' or censored by protest is that these protests are themselves protected acts of free speech. (This is why criticism is often directed at the hosting institution that is seen to have 'given in' to the protesters, rather than against the protesters themselves – although this is by no means always the case.) Likewise, if someone turns up to a public talk and shouts abuse from the audience, is that a limitation on free speech, or is it in fact an abundance of free speech? It depends, in part, on the nature of the abuse, and on whether the talk goes ahead regardless or has to be abandoned. But while it might be annoying to be heckled, it surely isn't an infringement of your civil rights. In fact, debates about no-platforming are about how we balance the competing but equally valid freedoms of two opposed parties, one of whom is in a position of institutionally conferred power – the invited speaker who has been given the floor – and the other whose power must somehow be summoned from elsewhere. The audience member who heckles a speaker is disrupting the accepted way of doing things; they are probably annoying the speaker, but they may also be annoying the other audience members as well. In other words, they are taking a big risk. No one asked them to speak, but they are doing so anyway. We would do well to ask ourselves why a person might resort to such behaviour.

The second factor to bear in mind is that debate itself has power: the power to discredit a point of view but also to legitimise and amplify it. Among those concerned for free speech on campus, 'debate' is seen as central to students' experience of university life. Despite the fact that in reality many students will go through university without ever seeking out or witnessing a formal debate, it is asserted that universities are places that should expose students to debates, and that students should participate in these rituals – both formally and informally – in order to experience the full force of opposing ideological positions and to learn how to defend their own positions. Many commentators valorise debate as a way – even the best way – to thrash out an argument and reach a set of shared principles and agreed ideas. And yet, debate assumes that both sides of an argument are worth listening to and that the truth can only be established by hearing them both out, and this is often simply not the case. Engineering students are no longer expected to debate the existence of the rules of gravity; biology students do not need to be exposed to 'both sides' of the argument of whether evolution really happens. These were once debates worth having, but today their scientific value is questionable at best. In the realm of politics and ethics, it is not hard to think of debates that might once have seemed worth having but are not any more: will child sacrifice placate the gods? Is it respectable to beat an enslaved person in public? Are women's brains capable of rational thought? The social and moral contexts of these debates have now changed. These are no longer questions that we would choose to air in public, because voicing them is offensive and potentially harmful to the people whose lives and identities are being questioned.

Furthermore, beyond the moral harms of these arguments, society does not need to continue to debate settled questions. We know that women are capable of rationality: we simply do not need to have any more discussions about it. Not only is it a waste of time to debate ideas that do not have two 'sides' – if someone really and truly does not believe that the Holocaust happened, for example, then a debate surely is not going to win them over – but it is also potentially harmful to platform, and thus gloss with a sheen of respectability, ideas that have been proven, time and time again, to be false. The principle behind no-platforming is the same as that behind the outlawing of Holocaust denial: debating ideas such as these has never killed them off, but it has frequently helped them to reach new audiences who might expect that they are worth considering simply by virtue of having been platformed at all.

We must also question the moral validity of debates about topics where, by definition, the stakes for those on one side of the argument are vastly greater than for those on the other. There is a clear difference between a speaker having an argument about gender identity or the experience of racism as an interesting theoretical debate, and a speaker having to defend their lived experience of their own identity to somebody who may not really know or care about their life. This difference is shaped by the identity of the person doing the speaking, the identity of the audience who are listening, and the influence of the speaker over wider policy: is the debate between two members of a marginalised group, in front of a sympathetic audience? Or is someone being paraded in front of a hostile crowd to defend their own lived experience? People have every right to refuse to participate in debates where they do not believe that the discussion is happening in good faith (or, even if it is, if they don't want to debate their position). But what if the debate taking place at all represents a violation, or even an act of rhetorical violence – what action is then legitimate?

Speech as violence

Jonathan Haidt and Greg Lukianoff, in an op-ed in *The Atlantic*, described the idea that 'speech is

sometimes violence' as possibly 'the most dangerous' idea on college campuses today.[66] The pair
were writing in the context of Milo Yiannopoulos'
campus speaking tour; Yiannopoulos had become
a poster boy for the 'alt right', a movement associated with racism, misogyny, homophobia and
even neo-Nazism. Yiannopoulos' speaking tour had
attracted significant protests and counter-protests,
most significantly at the University of California,
Berkeley, where violence had led to the cancellation
of the planned 'free speech week' that had intended
to platform a number of controversial right-wing
speakers.[67] Haidt and Lukianoff sought to dismiss
the idea that 'speech that is deemed by members
of an identity group to be critical of the group, or
speech that is otherwise upsetting to members
of the group' might itself constitute violence that
could therefore be legitimately shut down.

Haidt and Lukianoff were attempting to invali-
date an argument commonly used by left-wing
protesters to justify protest and de-platforming,
but also espoused by authors such as Lisa Feldman
Barrett, a psychology professor, who had written
in the *New York Times* that 'a culture of constant,
casual brutality is toxic to the body'. Feldman Barrett
had used this argument – based on neuroscientific

research into chronic stress – to propose that it was legitimate for students to refuse to allow a speaker who was primarily a 'provocateur and hatemonger' to visit their campus, because this hate speech itself was a form of casual brutality that would be experienced as toxic.[68] Of course, speech can *incite* violence; as Haidt and Lukianoff accepted, 'verbal threats of violence, which are used to coerce and intimidate' are 'illegal and not protected by the First Amendment'. But the idea that speech *itself* can also be experienced as violence is critical to making a moral case against every possible speech act being considered legitimate and worthy of protection.

In Toni Morrison's Nobel Lecture in 1993 she argued that 'Oppressive language does more than represent violence; it is violence.' Her description of the different forms of oppressive language includes 'sexist language, racist language, theistic language', which are all 'typical of the policing languages of mastery' and built on hierarchies of misogyny, racism, and other oppressions. The violence here is in the way that this language enacts these inequalities, rather than just describing them. Using racist language is itself a racist act; using a misogynist insult is itself misogynistic. It is not only that slurs can hurt or demean, although they can; it is also that using oppressive language is itself shoring up oppressive systems. The words cannot be separated from the sin.

Morrison spoke eloquently and presciently about how this 'language that drinks blood' is so dangerous, how it becomes part of polite discourse as it 'tucks its fascist boots under crinolines of respectability and patriotism'. But she argued too that we must fight hard to resist this language, not only because it is offensive, or even because it is dangerous – but because ultimately it does not 'permit new knowledge or encourage the mutual exchange of ideas'.[69] Morrison's point is that the language of oppression – speech as violence – is not only harmful to the listener who is hurt by it (both morally and also potentially physically, as Feldman Barrett's work has shown). It is also inimical to the very thing that debate supposedly provides: the arrival at new insight via dialectical means. People cannot engage in productive, generative discussion when the tone and language of that discussion are hostile to their very existence. And vulnerable or minoritised groups cannot be expected to do important critical, philosophical work in an environment that is draining, bruising or abusive. In this sense, when people protest in order to shut down this form of language they are not limiting free speech but working to open up society to the possibility of more freedoms, for more people.

In *The Identity Trap* (2023), Yascha Mounk argues that the progressive left has become problematically focused on discourse: 'In virtually every developed democracy, activists now expend enormous efforts on changing the way in which ordinary people speak.'[70] But in this context, it is not clear why attempting to change the language used to discuss particular topics, or to stigmatise the use of (for example) slurs against specific groups, or to interrupt or prevent talks by people who are planning to use harmful or hateful language, is something that should be alarming. In fact, trying to make sure that hateful or harmful language is avoided seems more like a moral good, not least because it creates space for more people to feel included in debate.

This accusation that the left is overly fixated with the way that people speak is not new. As the Thatcher years unfolded in Britain – and prefiguring the recent culture wars in Britain under Johnson, Truss and Sunak – there was a growing obsession in the right-wing press with the idea of 'political correctness gone mad'. At its heart was the idea that sensitivity to offensive language was being taken to absurd extremes and thus becoming a form of political oppression. British newspaper stories and jokey rumours proliferated about 'loony left' councils refusing to refer to 'black bin bags' or 'black coffee'; there was a huge media scandal when it transpired that a working group on racism in children's resources for Birmingham City Council had advised a nursery school not to use the word 'black' as a negative label – 'Black Monday', 'black sheep' – and suggested that 'there are other nursery rhymes for children to sing'.[71] Making fun of progressive censoriousness may be amusing to some – and, in some people's view, it may even be necessary – but it is not a victimless pursuit. The mockery and panic had real-world consequences: the 1988 introduction of Section 28, which forbade local authorities and schools from 'promoting homosexuality', was arguably a response to a creeping unease among right-wing elites that they were losing the war for cultural norms and mores.[72] If much of the defence of 'free speech' against cancellation is really a defence of the right to say specific, morally unacceptable things, the mockery of the idea that speech can be violent or oppressive is sometimes really a defence of the right to attack or oppress specific vulnerable groups. There is a moral case for 'cancellation'; some speech is dangerous and some speakers *should* be shamed for what they choose to say.

Conclusion: more freedom, less speech

Those who argue that freedom of speech is under threat too often disregard the unequal way that speech is used and experienced. It is far easier to speak your truth if you do not have to worry about what others think, and it is far easier to live without approval if you have the power to resist criticism or the means to go it alone. Historically, it has always been those with power who have found it easiest to speak their minds without meaningful opposition. For most people, the problem has been making themselves heard at all. Social media has changed this significantly in some ways, but only a minority have access to the publishing and broadcasting apparatus that still has the power to lend a speaker serious authority and credibility and influence.

Those who argue that free speech is under threat too often dance around the actual words being said and treat speech in the abstract. But speech is an action, not an abstraction. And speaking is not only something you do, it is something you do *to others*. A speaker commands, demands, requests, pleads and asserts; those who listen will at some level be affected, for good or ill, whether they like it or not. The law recognises this, which is why inciting violence is a criminal act, regardless of whether violence occurs. Free speech advocates often defend offensive speech as brave, but there is nothing brave about using your relative power and position to attack and perhaps endanger a person or group more vulnerable than you are. Even Orwell, in his defence of free speech, qualified this freedom: 'everyone shall have the right to say and to print what he believes to be the truth, *provided only that it does not harm the rest of the community in some quite unmistakable way*.'[73]

Many of the loudest voices about free speech tend also to skate over the fact that censorship – real censorship, the kind that we should be genuinely worried about – is something done by governments and states. If we take international law as our guide, it is intrinsic to the concept of censorship that it is an abuse specifically of *state* power, in order to control political realities and to shut down opposition. It is about controlling what can be said in order to control what can be known. One of the gravest effects of the current panic about freedom of speech is that by focusing on the progressive censoriousness of teenage university students, we are paying less attention to the ways that governments might actually be limiting people's right to protest, or to express political opinions, without censure or reprisals.

In 2023, the then Home Secretary Suella Braverman argued that waving a Palestinian flag, or repeating the chant 'from the river to the sea, Palestine will be free', could constitute a criminal offence.[74] During the coronation of King Charles III, Just Stop Oil protesters were arrested for wearing T-shirts presenting their affiliation with the group; a number of members of the campaign group Republic, including the chief executive Graham Smith, were arrested because they were wearing T-shirts proclaiming 'Not My King'.[75] However offensive or even frightening some may find these acts of protest, such arrests, both real and putative, are and would be actual infringements of freedom of speech in the UK, because they are actions taken by the state against those protesting its power. But there has been little outcry about them from the right-wing press, because they do not map onto the prevailing anxieties about cancel culture.

In a similar way, the concern that university campuses have become a space where freedom of speech is being attacked has become a way of monitoring and attempting to control what is happening in higher education in Britain. Newspapers have increasingly used freedom of information requests as a way to monitor 'woke' academics and report on their use of trigger warnings and efforts to 'decolonise' their curricula. Such actions are portrayed as encroachments on or erosions of freedom of speech: trigger warnings are seen as evidence that you can't say anything any more, while the removal of texts from reading lists is presented as an erasure of certain writers and perspectives from the canon. From an academic perspective, trigger warnings and content notes actually enable a wider group of students to participate in discussions on sensitive topics; removing texts from reading lists is done to make space for alternatives, which have mostly been less studied and represent a more diverse array of voices and perspectives. Neither of these is a free speech issue. However, the continual surveillance of university staff and students by a section of the UK media does itself have a chilling effect on academic freedom.

George Orwell's essay, the unpublished preface

to *Animal Farm*, is perhaps best known for the line, 'If liberty means anything at all it means the right to tell people what they do not want to hear', a phrase often used by defenders of free speech to argue that even the most unpopular speech must still be permitted. But the same axiom might also be used to argue that a person's defence of free speech is only really meaningful when it is made on behalf of a person whose views you disagree with; that is surely the real test of a person's commitment to free speech in all circumstances. On this basis, today's free speech defenders are often part-time warriors, concerned primarily with certain types of speech and speakers and less quick to defend others. Anxieties about cancel culture and freedom of speech and the sense that you 'can't say anything any more' are really anxieties about social change, and the slipping away of old power structures to be replaced with new ones. Freedom of speech, which is often proclaimed as a pillar of democracy, and the upholding of which is vital in order to protect the most powerless in society, is in reality often weaponised in order to maintain the status quo, and to bolster the power of the most powerful.

This weaponisation takes various forms but boils down in the end to the same thing: the mislabelling of criticism as silencing. Of course, sometimes critique is an attempt to silence people, to neutralise or rebut someone's views to the point that no one takes them seriously any more. And sometimes, yes, it takes the form of telling people to shut up. But is this *silencing*? Is it 'cancellation'? Or is it simply part of having a conversation? Perhaps those who do not want to be criticised or told to shut up are people who have, historically, found themselves most easily able to make themselves heard; when you have always been able to speak without interruption, even the mildest heckle might feel like a dangerous blow. In the end, it is profoundly unserious to respond to criticism of your views by claiming that your speech is being threatened or that you are being 'cancelled'. In fact, far from cancel culture meaningfully attacking conservative speech, the *outcry* about cancel culture is almost always aimed at shutting down progressive speech.

We shouldn't let it. Marginalised groups are less likely to be given platforms for their ideas, less likely to find support to develop their writing and their advocacy, and less likely to be defended against criticism and attack. Women of colour face significantly more attempts to shut down their speech on the internet than white men; wealthy elites are more likely to have the social and cultural connections that enable them to get newspaper columns and book deals. And yet we are living in a moment where people have more ability to broadcast their ideas globally than ever before: the internet has been enormously democratising in terms of who gets to speak and who is able to listen. Some of this democracy, to the people who are used to speaking without rebuttal, might feel alarming. But cancel culture is, often, simply the anger of the previously unheard becoming audible: the freedom of speech for more people, at a higher volume than ever before. 'Progressive censoriousness' is in fact a feature of free speech, not a bug: it is what happens when speech is exposed to more perspectives and when the right to respond is given to a greater number of people.

Turn this book over to read the alternative view.

Notes

1. It was later published in the October issue of the magazine. 'A Letter on Justice and Open Debate', *Harper's*, 7 July 2020: https://harpers.org/a-letter-on-justice-and-open-debate/

2. 'Artists and Writers Warn of an "Intolerant Climate." Reaction Is Swift', *New York Times*, 7 July 2020: https://www.nytimes.com/2020/07/07/arts/harpers-letter.html

3. Paul Berman, 'Lynching and Liberalism', *Tablet*, 17 August 2020: https://www.tabletmag.com/sections/arts-letters/articles/liberalism-harpers-letter-dewey

4. 'The cancel-culture fightback: how the "Harper's letter" astonished the Twitter mob', *Daily Telegraph*, 15 July 2020: https://www.telegraph.co.uk/books/news/cancel-culture-fightback-harpers-letter-astonished-twitter-mob/

5. Laura Bradley, 'J.K. Rowling and Other Assorted Rich Fools Want to Cancel "Cancel Culture"', *Daily Beast*, 7 July 2020: https://www.thedailybeast.com/jk-rowling-and-other-assorted-rich-fools-want-to-cancel-cancel-culture

6. Chloe Laws, 'J. K. Rowling, it's not "cancel culture" that's led to people withdrawing their support for you, here's what has . . .', *Glamour*, 8 July 2002:

https://www.glamourmagazine.co.uk/article/jk-rowling-cancel-culture

7. Cara Buckley, 'New York Review of Books Editor Is Out Amid Uproar Over #MeToo Essay', *New York Times*, 19 September 2018: https://www.nytimes.com/2018/09/19/arts/ian-buruma-out-jian-ghomeshi.html

8. 'A More Specific Letter on Justice and Open Debate', *The Objective*, 10 July 2020: https://objectivejournalism.org/2020/07/a-more-specific-letter-on-justice-and-open-debate

9. Deirdre Nansen McCloskey, 'I'm a transwoman who signed the Harper's letter with J K Rowling. Here's why', *Prospect*, 13 August 2020: https://www.prospectmagazine.co.uk/culture/40480/im-a-transwoman-who-signed-the-harpers-letter-with-jk-rowling.-heres-why

10. 'A More Specific Letter on Justice and Open Debate', *The Objective*, 10 July 2020: https://objectivejournalism.org/2020/07/a-more-specific-letter-on-justice-and-open-debate/

11. Theresa May, 'A Stronger Britain, Built On Our Values', speech delivered to Royal Institute of Chartered Surveyors, 23 March 2015: https://www.gov.uk/government/speeches/a-stronger-britain-built-on-our-values

12. 'Woke' is an appropriation of African-American Vernacular English (AAVE); see Domenico Montanaro, 'What does the word "woke" really mean, and where does it come from?', NPR, 19 July 2023: https://www.npr.org/2023/07/19/1188543449/what-does-the-word-woke-really-mean-and-where-does-it-come-from

13. Henry Irving and Judith Townend, 'Censorship and National Security: Information Control in the Second World War and Present Day', *History and Policy*,

10 February 2016: https://www.historyandpolicy.org/
policy-papers/papers/censorship-and-national-security-
information-control

14. Jane Hapman, Anna Hoyles, Andrew Kerr, Adam
    Sherif, 'Collective Culture as Dynamic Record: The
    Daily Worker, 1940–43', in *Comics and the World Wars: A
    Cultural Record*, Palgrave Macmillan, 2015, p. 150

15. See, for example, Robert Darnton, 'Literary Surveillance
    in the British Raj: The Contradictions of Liberal Imperial-
    ism', *Book History*, Vol. 4, 2001, pp. 133–76; Emma Larkin,
    'The Self-Conscious Censor: Censorship in Burma under
    the British, 1900–1939', *Journal of Burma Studies*, Vol. 8,
    2003, pp. 64–101; Charles Ambler, 'Popular Films and
    Colonial Audiences: The Movies in Northern Rhodesia',
    American Historical Review, Vol. 106, No. 1, 2001, p. 92

16. Richard J. Evans, *Telling Lies About Hitler: The Holocaust,
    History and the David Irving Trial*, Verso, 2002, p. 266

17. Alice Sandham, 'Denial: An Interview with Sir Richard
    Evans', Woolf Institute, 7 February 2017: https://www.
    woolf.cam.ac.uk/blog/denial-an-interview-with-sir-
    richard-evans

18. 'David Irving jailed for Holocaust denial', *Guardian*,
    20 February 2006: https://www.theguardian.com/
    world/2006/feb/20/austria.thefarright; 'Unrepenting
    Denier', Deutsche Welle, 22 December 2006: https://
    www.dw.com/en/convicted-holocaust-denier-irving-
    expelled-from-austria/a-2288055

19. Kate Connolly, 'Holocaust denial writer jailed for
    five years', *Guardian*, 16 February 2007: https://www.
    theguardian.com/world/2007/feb/16/historybooks.
    secondworldwar

20. 'Holocaust denier Fredrick Toben jailed in Australia',
    Daily Telegraph, 14 August 2009: https://www.telegraph.

co.uk/news/worldnews/australiaandthepacific/
australia/6025275/Holocaust-denier-Fredrick-Toben-
jailed-in-Australia.html

21. George Orwell, 'The Freedom of the Press', *c.*1945,
proposed preface to *Animal Farm*, *Times Literary
Supplement*, 15 September 1972, reprinted by The Orwell
Foundation: https://www.orwellfoundation.com/the-
orwell-foundation/orwell/essays-and-other-works/
the-freedom-of-the-press/

22. Ibid.

23. Kelsey Koberg, 'The woke mob is everywhere: Here's
where it came from and how one critic believes it can be
stopped', Fox News, 24 July 2021: https://www.foxnews.
com/media/the-woke-mob-is-everywhere-heres-where-
it-came-from-and-victor-davis-hansons-solution-for-
stopping-it

24. Piers Morgan, 'I said to Rebekah Vardy: "I'm here to repair
your public image!"', *MailOnline*, 16 November 2019:
https://www.dailymail.co.uk/home/event/article-7684975/
I-said-Rebekah-Vardy-Im-repair-public-image.html

25. Mark Remy, 'Ways the Woke Mob Has Offended Me
Personally', *New Yorker*, 25 June 2022: https://www.
newyorker.com/humor/daily-shouts/ways-the-woke-
mob-has-affected-me-personally

26. William L. Sachse, 'The Mob and the Revolution of
1688', *Journal of British Studies*, Vol. 4, No. 1, 1964, p. 23

27. Amia Srinivasan, 'Cancelled', *London Review of Books*,
Vol. 45, No. 13, 29 June 2023: https://www.lrb.co.uk/the-
paper/v45/n13/amia-srinivasan/cancelled

28. J. R. Shackleton (ed.), *Having your say: Threats to free
speech in the 21st century*, IEA, 20 June 2021: https://iea.
org.uk/publications/having-your-say-threats-to-free-
speech-in-the-21st-century/; Christopher Snowden, 'The

Nanny State Index '23': https://nannystateindex.org/
nanny-state-criteria-2023/

29. Samira Shackle, 'The backlash: how slavery research came
under fire', *Guardian*, 1 June 2023: https://www.theguardian.
com/news/2023/jun/01/cotton-capital-legacies-of-slavery-
research-backlash-cambridge-university

30. Bruce Gilley, 'The Case for Colonialism', reprinted in
National Association of Scholars, *Academic Questions*,
Summer 2018: https://www.nas.org/academic-
questions/31/2/the_case_for_colonialism

31. Bruce Gilley, 'The Case for Colonialism', *Third World
Quarterly*, 2017: https://doi.org/10.1080/01436597.2017.13
69037

32. Nigel Biggar, 'Don't feel guilty about our colonial
history', *The Times*, 30 November 2017: https://
www.thetimes.com/article/
don-t-feel-guilty-about-our-colonial-history-ghvstdhmj

33. Colleen Flaherty, 'Resignations at "Third World
Quarterly"', *Inside Higher Ed*, 19 September 2017: https://
www.insidehighered.com/news/2017/09/20/much-
third-world-quarterlys-editorial-board-resigns-saying-
controversial-article

34. 'Oxford Continues to Defend Colonialism at Every
Opportunity – A Response from Common Ground',
Common Ground Oxford, n.d.: https://
commongroundoxford.wordpress.com/response-to-
nigel-biggars-article-dont-feel-guilty-about-our-colonial-
history/

35. 'Ethics and empire: an open letter from Oxford scholars',
The Conversation, 19 December 2017: http://theconver
sation.com/ethics-and-empire-an-open-letter-from-
oxford-scholars-89333

36. David Brown, 'Oxford backs academic Nigel Biggar over

"bigoted" views', *The Times*, 16 December 2017: https://www.thetimes.com/uk/education/article/oxford-backs-academic-nigel-biggar-over-bigoted-views-nffdfxnjv

37. Nigel Biggar, 'Political discrimination should be as unacceptable as racism at universities', *Daily Telegraph*, 8 August 2020: https://www.telegraph.co.uk/men/thinking-man/political-discrimination-should-unacceptable-racism-universities/

38. David Sanderson, 'Campus censorship is Stalinist, says Oxford professor Nigel Biggar', *The Times*, 8 October 2018: https://www.thetimes.com/uk/education/article/campus-censorship-is-stalinist-says-oxford-professor-nigel-biggar-5870pt28f

39. Camilla Turner, 'Academics fear being "mobbed" if they stand up for the British Empire, Oxford scholar says', *Daily Telegraph*, 20 June 2020: https://www.telegraph.co.uk/news/2020/06/20/academics-fear-mobbed-stand-british-empire-oxford-scholar-says/

40. Bruce Gilley, 'How the Hate Mob Tried to Silence Me', *Standpoint Magazine*, December 2017, reprinted at Middle East Forum Campus Watch: https://www.meforum.org/campus-watch/25424/how-the-hate-mob-tried-to-silence-me-incl-hamid

41. '"This climate of cancel culture – this illiberal climate – has happened very quickly." Cancelled professor Nigel Biggar tells Neil Oliver "open" universities have been replaced by a culture of "caution and fear"', tweet published by GB News, 24 July 2021: https://x.com/GBNEWS/status/1419019741222612996; Simon Heffer, 'Nigel Biggar: the Oxford professor ostracised for defending the Empire', *Daily Telegraph*, 23 February 2019: https://www.telegraph.co.uk/men/thinking-man/nigel-biggar-oxford-professor-ostracised-defending-empire

42. Andrew Ellson, 'Nigel Biggar Hits Out over 'Cancelled' book on Empire', The Times, 28 January 2023: https://www.thetimes.com/culture/books/article/nigel-biggar-hits-out-bloomsbury-cancelled-book-empire-8s75506dk

43. Nigel Biggar, 'The publishing industry is killing free speech and spreading lies – by cancelling authors like me', *MailOnline*, 4 February 2023: https://www.dailymail.co.uk/columnists/article-11711995/The-publishing-industry-killing-free-speech-spreading-lies-cancelling-authors-like-me.html

44. Jack Malvern, Matt Dathan, Henry Zeffman, 'Queen's birthday honours: Nigel Biggar appointed CBE after storm over his colonial views', *The Times*, 12 June 2021: https://www.thetimes.co.uk/article/queen-s-birthday-honours-nigel-biggar-appointed-cbe-after-storm-over-his-colonial-views-rzs7c9jbp

45. Bryan Pietsch, 'Massachusetts Detective Is Fired Over Black Lives Matter Post', *New York Times*, 5 July 2020: https://www.nytimes.com/2020/07/05/us/Black-lives-matter-detective-fired-Springfield.html; Stuti Mishra and Press Association, 'British doctor suspended over involvement in Just Stop Oil protests', *Independent*, 24 April 2024: https://www.independent.co.uk/climate-change/news/climate-protest-uk-doctor-suspended-b2533788.html

46. Madison Malone Kircher, 'Study Finds Twitter Is Bad If You're a Woman and Worse If You're a Woman of Color', *New York Magazine*, 18 December 2018: https://nymag.com/intelligencer/2018/12/study-finds-black-women-on-twitter-face-more-abuse.html; Carolina Caeiro and Carolina Tchintian, 'Tackling online abuse against women politicians', *World Today*, 2 November 2021: https://www.chathamhouse.org/publications/

the-world-today/2021-10/tackling-online-
abuse-against-women-politicians

47. 'Full text: Michael Howard's speech', *Guardian*,
28 January 2005: https://www.theguardian.com/
politics/2005/jan/28/conservatives.uk; Priti Patel,
'Home Secretary Priti Patel speech on immigration',
speech delivered to Bright Blue and British Future, 24
May 2021: https://www.gov.uk/government/speeches/
home-secretary-priti-patel-speech-on-immigration

48. Neha Gohil, 'Scrap trigger warnings for theatre
audiences, says Ralph Fiennes', *Guardian*, 11 February
2024: https://www.theguardian.com/stage/2024/feb/11/
ralph-fiennes-scrap-trigger-warnings-for-theatre-
audiences; Nicole Vassell, 'Matt Smith weighs in on
theatre trigger warning debate: "Isn't art meant to be
dangerous?"', *Independent*, 20 February 2024: https://
www.independent.co.uk/arts-entertainment/theatre-
dance/news/matt-smith-trigger-warning-b2499102.html

49. 'We will not bail out universities in financial difficulty,
regulator chair says', Office for Students, 6 November
2018: https://www.officeforstudents.org.uk/news-blog-
and-events/press-and-media/we-will-not-bail-out-
universities-in-financial-difficulty-regulator-chair-says/

50. Charlotte Lytton, 'The cancelled professor launching the
UK's first "anti-woke" university course', *Daily Telegraph*,
10 October 2023: https://www.telegraph.co.uk/
education-and-careers/2023/10/10/birkbeck-university-
anti-woke-course-free-speech/

51. 'Militants and Moderates in the Universities', *Minerva*,
Vol. 7, No. 1/2, Autumn–Winter 1968–69, pp. 284–300

52. Ibid.

53. Alison D. Graham, 'International Crises: Penn's
Involvement in the Global Conflicts in the 20th Century',

A Brief History of Global Engagement at the University of Pennsylvania, n.d.: https://archives.upenn.edu/exhibits/penn-history/global-engagement/international-crises/vietnam-war/

54. Evan Smith, 'A Policy Widely Abused: The Origins of the "No Platform" Policy of the National Union of Students', *History and Policy*, 23 March 2016: https://www.historyandpolicy.org/opinion-articles/articles/a-policy-widely-abused

55. Priyamvada Gopal, 'Statement on Home Office Cancellation of my Talk on Anticolonialism, Race, and Empire', Medium, 14 October 2021: https://zen-catgirl.medium.com/statement-on-home-office-cancellation-of-my-talk-on-anticolonialism-race-and-empire-e52cf149ec81; Chas Geiger, 'Government apologises to barred weapons expert Dan Kaszeta', BBC News, 12 July 2023: https://www.bbc.co.uk/news/uk-politics-66180552; Anna Fazackerley, 'Revealed: UK government keeping files on education critics' social media activity', *Guardian*, 30 September 2023: https://www.theguardian.com/education/2023/sep/30/revealed-uk-government-keeping-files-on-education-critics-social-media-activity

56. Jamie Grierson, 'Amber Rudd hits out at "rude" Oxford students after talk cancelled', *Guardian*, 6 March 2020: https://www.theguardian.com/politics/2020/mar/06/amber-rudd-hits-out-at-rude-oxford-students-after-talk-cancelled

57. Lucy Campbell, 'Free speech row at Oxford University after Rudd talk cancelled', *Guardian*, 6 March 2020: https://www.theguardian.com/politics/2020/mar/06/free-speech-row-at-oxford-university-after-amber-rudd-talk-cancelled

58. Jamie Grierson, 'Amber Rudd hits out at "rude" Oxford

students after talk cancelled', *Guardian*, 6 March 2020: https://www.theguardian.com/politics/2020/mar/06/amber-rudd-hits-out-at-rude-oxford-students-after-talk-cancelled

59. Martin Belam, 'Toby Young quotes on breasts, eugenics and working-class people', *Guardian*, 3 January 2018: https://www.theguardian.com/media/2018/jan/03/toby-young-quotes-on-breasts-eugenics-and-working-class-people; Richard Adams, 'Toby Young: how barrage of nudges made OfS position untenable', *Guardian*, 9 January 2018: https://www.theguardian.com/education/2018/jan/09/toby-young-how-barrage-of-nudges-made-ofs-position-untenable

60. Paul Waugh, 'Ministers Preparing New Law To "Protect Freedom Of Speech" At Universities', *HuffPost*, 7 March 2020: https://www.huffingtonpost.co.uk/entry/gavin-williamson-new-law-freedom-of-speech-university-oxford_uk_5e63fa78c5b6670e72f90ef5

61. 'Freedom of Speech Act: How it will affect university students', The Education Hub (Department of Education), 30 May 2023: https://educationhub.blog.gov.uk/2023/05/30/freedom-of-speech-act-how-it-will-affect-university-students/

62. Rob Merrick, 'No 10 slaps down universities minister for saying "Free Speech Bill" will allow Holocaust deniers to speak', *Independent*, 13 May 2021: https://www.independent.co.uk/news/uk/politics/holocaust-denial-universities-michele-donelan-b1846924.html

63. Richard Adams, 'Campus free speech law in England "likely to have opposite effect"', *Guardian*, 12 May 2021: https://www.theguardian.com/education/2021/may/12/campus-free-speech-law-england-likely-opposite-effect

64. Eric Kaufmann, 'The Freedom of Speech Bill is a

huge step towards saving the soul of university education', *Daily Telegraph*, 12 May 2021: https://www.telegraph.co.uk/news/2021/05/12/freedom-speech-bill-bid-save-soul-university-education/

65. Amia Srinivasan, 'Cancelled', *London Review of Books*, Vol. 45, No. 13, 29 June 2023: https://www.lrb.co.uk/the-paper/v45/n13/amia-srinivasan/cancelled

66. Jonathan Haidt and Greg Lukianoff, 'Why It's a Bad Idea to Tell Students Words Are Violence', *The Atlantic*, 18 July 2017: https://www.theatlantic.com/education/archive/2017/07/why-its-a-bad-idea-to-tell-students-words-are-violence/533970/

67. Phil McCausland and Yelena Dzhanova, '"Free Speech Week" at UC Berkeley Canceled, Milo Yiannopoulos Blames School', NBC News, 23 September 2017: https://www.nbcnews.com/news/us-news/free-speech-week-uc-berkeley-canceled-milo-yiannopoulos-blames-school-n804171

68. Lisa Feldman Barrett, 'When Is Speech Violence?', *New York Times*, 14 July 2017: https://www.nytimes.com/2017/07/14/opinion/sunday/when-is-speech-violence.html

69. Toni Morrison, Nobel Lecture, 7 December 1993: https://www.nobelprize.org/prizes/literature/1993/morrison/lecture/

70. Yascha Mounk, *The Identity Trap: A Story of Ideas and Power in Our Time*, Allen Lane, 2023, p. 67

71. Sean O'Grady, 'The truth about political correctness – in black and white', *Independent*, 26 September 2002: https://www.independent.co.uk/news/uk/home-news/analysis-the-truth-about-political-correctness-in-black-and-white-131925.html

72. John Vincent, 'Political correctness', in Dave Muddiman,

Shiraz Durrani, Martin Dutch, Rebecca Linley, John Pateman and John Vincent (eds), *Open to All? The Public Library and Social Exclusion, Volume Three: Working Papers,* Council for Museums, Archives and Libraries, 2000, pp. 350–61

73. George Orwell, 'The Freedom of the Press', *c.*1945, proposed preface to *Animal Farm, Times Literary Supplement*, 15 September 1972, reprinted by The Orwell Foundation: https://www.orwellfoundation.com/the-orwell-foundation/orwell/essays-and-other-works/the-freedom-of-the-press/ (italics my own)

74. Rajeev Syal and Aubrey Allegretti, 'Waving Palestinian flag may be a criminal offence, Braverman tells police', *Guardian*, 10 October 2023: https://www.theguardian.com/politics/2023/oct/10/people-supporting-hamas-in-uk-will-be-held-to-account-says-rishi-sunak

75. Chloe Naldrett, 'Arrested for wearing a T-shirt? The coronation heralded a frightening slide towards authoritarianism', *Guardian*, 7 May 2023: https://www.theguardian.com/commentisfree/2023/may/07/coronation-just-stop-oil-republic-activists-peaceful-protests; Daniel Boffey and Nicola Slawson, 'Police accused of "alarming" attack on protest rights after anti-monarchist leader arrested', *Guardian*, 7 May 2023: https://www.theguardian.com/uk-news/2023/may/06/head-of-uks-leading-anti-monarchy-group-arrested-at-coronation-protest

Suzanne Nossel is the CEO of PEN America, the leading human rights and free expression organisation, and is a key voice on free expression issues in the United States and globally. During the Obama administration, Nossel served as Deputy Assistant Secretary of State for International Organisations. She has also served as a senior leader in global human rights organisations and as a media executive. She is the author of *Dare To Speak: Defending Free Speech For All* and has been widely published in outlets including the *New York Times*, *Foreign Affairs*, *Guardian*, *Foreign Policy*, *Wall Street Journal*, *TIME*, *Washington Post* and more. She is a Member of the Meta Oversight Board which applies human rights principles to shape high impact content moderation decisions on social media.

Is Free Speech
Under Threat?

SUZANNE NOSSEL

1 3 5 7 9 10 8 6 4 2

The Bodley Head, an imprint of Vintage, is part of the
Penguin Random House group of companies whose addresses
can be found at global.penguinrandomhouse.com

Penguin
Random House
UK

First published by the Bodley Head in 2024

penguin.co.uk/vintage

Typeset in 13.3/18.2pt Calluna by Jouve (UK), Milton Keynes
Printed and bound in Great Britain by Clays Ltd, Elcograf S.p.A.

The authorised representative in the EEA is Penguin Random House
Ireland, Morrison Chambers, 32 Nassau Street, Dublin D02 YH68

A CIP catalogue record for this book is available from the British Library

ISBN 9781847928221

Penguin Random House is committed to a sustainable future
for our business, our readers and our planet. This book is
made from Forest Stewardship Council® certified paper.

Is Free Speech Under Threat?

Is Free Speech Under Threat?

During the 2023–24 school year, many of the United States' most prestigious universities erupted. The protests, chants, encampments and confrontations centred on the war between Israel and Hamas. But they also implicated tensions closer to home. Slogans like 'from the river to the sea' or 'intifada revolution' were heard by some as an empowering rallying cry for Palestinian solidarity, and by others as a call for ethnic elimination of Jews. To some, the encampments were part of a noble tradition of valiant protest harking back to the Vietnam War and the anti-apartheid movement focused on South Africa. To others, they were a menacing manifestation of rising foreign influence, involving off-campus movements paid to radicalise American youth. To some, the protests were an impassioned plea to save innocent lives, foster peace and elevate

the sanctity of humanity. To others, they were an effort to delegitimise and demonise a vulnerable people, paving the way towards their annihilation.

The protests brought into view and deepened a crisis of confidence in the bedrock American precept – enshrined in nearly one hundred years of jurisprudence on the First Amendment to the US Constitution – that even the most controversial and provocative speech merits protection, and that the best answer to noxious speech is refutation through more speech.* Some claimed that efforts to curtail the largely peaceful protests were a betrayal of free speech precepts – a form of viewpoint-based repression aimed to silence dissident perspectives. Others argued that enforcing university restrictions on when, where and how protests could be carried out was simply a way to safeguard the rights of all and prevent disruption to the essential functions of the campus as a place for teaching and learning. Off-campus forces – whether wealthy donors or well-resourced international advocacy campaigns – were blamed for illegitimately skewing the debates.

---

* While the First Amendment only governs speech at public institutions of higher education, most private universities have voluntarily adopted policies and approaches that aim to offer commensurate protections for expression.

Students and faculty argued that rules governing who could speak and when were being applied unfairly: some said pro-Palestinian speech was being unjustly targeted while others argued that Jewish students were being subjected to hateful speech that would not be tolerated were it directed towards other historically marginalised groups. The disputes were exacerbated by outdated university policies including regulations that were on the books but had long gone unenforced.

Leaders and administrators were flummoxed over how to uphold free speech rights without allowing their campuses to become places of menace and intimidation for certain students. Age-old traumas on all sides bred heightened ardour and intensified feelings of vulnerability. Meanwhile, students on many campuses reported that actual debate on the history, consequences or moral weight of the Israel–Hamas conflict was all but impossible. Classmates were afraid to voice their views except in sheltered enclaves of the like-minded. Seminar-room discussions were stilted for fear of offending someone or, worse still, being captured in a viral video that could haunt a future career.

The uproar fuelled the resignations of the presidents of Harvard and the University of Pennsylvania,

the withdrawal of hundreds of millions of dollars in donations to leading colleges, the initiation of Congressional and state legislative investigations, multiple probes by state and federal civil rights agencies, lawsuits accusing leading universities of turning a blind eye to bigotry and harassment, and complaints to educational accreditation agencies.[1] Meanwhile, similar student movements including solidarity encampments began popping up on campuses around the world: at Trinity College in Dublin, Lausanne University in Switzerland, Sciences Po in Paris, the University of the Witwatersrand in South Africa and elsewhere.

These campus clashes reflect a set of tensions roiling increasingly diverse, social media-soaked societies, as institutions of all kinds navigate between accommodating the needs of a heterogeneous population, and the legal and communal values of free speech and open discourse. In the past decade, media organisations, corporations, technology platforms and civic groups have wrestled with dilemmas over the changing bounds of acceptable speech, and how those limits should be determined and enforced. Among conservatives and some liberals, there are those who believe that topics including immigration, gender identity, gun

control, and the role of race in society have been ring-fenced by left-wing orthodoxies that allow little space for opposing perspectives. Incensed by what they see as ideological rigidities dominating a growing swathe of elite institutions – universities, national news organisations and major consumer brands – some conservatives have fought back with approaches including, in the US, bans on books, and legislated prohibitions on school and higher education curricula. Paradoxically, such measures are not reinforcements of the liberty their proponents maintain is being eroded, but rather government-backed constraints that curtail and punish speech.

The fireworks on US campuses were the culmination of an escalating free speech arms race, with constituencies on the left and the right pressing for disfavoured opinions to be declared out of bounds, socially, morally or legally. The more each side comes to believe that the opposing flank is notching gains in its quest to curtail speech that it abhors, the more determined each becomes to retaliate in kind, declaring new no-go areas and prohibitions. Hypocrisy abounds, with voices on both left and right decrying one another for cancelling disfavoured voices, drowning out dissent, or for wilfully disregarding what they claim are grave

harms and dangers that speech may cause. While the tactics on the right and left differ, and power differentials shape the import of their efforts, both sides have resorted to speech protective tactics in service of their ideological aims.

Given the United States' historic status as a global free speech standard-bearer, with the First Amendment to the Constitution marking the most protective legal regime for speech anywhere in the world, the deepening divides over what free speech means and how it should be protected in the US reverberate globally. And indeed the 'cancellation' of those who voice controversial views, book bans targeting LGBTQ narratives, efforts to discipline professors for errant speech, and the patrolling of speech on the Israel–Hamas conflict are not limited to the United States. In 2023 the United Kingdom's Conservative government appointed Cambridge philosophy professor Arif Ahmed as the nation's first 'free speech tsar' to focus on defending free speech and academic freedom from mounting threats.[2] In early 2024 the French parliament passed a new law that would 'strengthen the criminal response to racist or antisemitic offences' and render such speech subject to 'a guaranteed and systematic criminal penalty'.[3] The repression of pro-Palestinian

speech in the art and cultural world in Germany has sparked uproar, raising questions of how to reconcile the country's history of genocide with its present-day values of liberalism and openness to dissent.[4] Elsewhere in Europe, conference convenors and academic departments have shunned Israeli scholars and institutions, cutting off dialogue and exchange with independent voices because of anger over actions by the Israeli government.

Compounding doubts, confusion and disputes over free speech on campus and in culture is a widespread sense that, online, expression has run amok. Propelled by algorithmic amplification and jet-fuelled by profit motives, digital discourse is increasingly recognised as posing a danger to public health, mental wellbeing, social cohesion and democracy itself. The bipartisan April 2024 vote in the United States Congress to force TikTok to sell itself or shut down in the US reflected escalating alarm over how online discourse may threaten national security. The concerns relate to TikTok's links to the Chinese government and fears that the platform is a uniquely effective and shadowy vehicle for the manipulation of opinion. TikTok, with the support of certain leading free speech groups, is mounting a First Amendment challenge to the law.[5]

With pitfalls and challenges arrayed on all sides, free speech is losing its moorings on both the right and the left. Some argue that the costs of free speech borne by historically marginalised groups are simply too high. Others claim almost the opposite: that free speech rights are being exercised in ways that distort and override majority opinions and mainstream cultural values. Critics of free speech safeguards maintain that such restraints leave society too exposed to those who exploit discourse in the name of money or power. Free speech is dismissed as a plaything for special interests or a principle that is too easily contorted as cover for other less noble goals. The defence of free speech is denigrated as a smokescreen for hatred, a veil for ideological agendas or a legitimiser of violence. These concerns are not idle. Free speech principles can be invoked selectively, distorted or misused. But that is a reason to redouble the defence of a principled approach to free speech, rather than give in to the forces that would pervert it.

Given the United States' historic role as a citadel for free speech, the challenges on American quadrangles, bookshelves, streets and social media have the potential to reshape the meaning of free expression ideals globally. This perilous situation could prompt liberty-loving citizenries to reckon with new threats

to free speech and renew their vows to uphold it as a sacred value. Or it could hasten resort to suppressive tactics justified in the name of other interests, tilting democratic societies towards authoritarianism. To paraphrase what Winston Churchill once said about democracy, and as dissidents in China, Russia and Iran would roundly confirm – a polity that protects free speech is the worst form of society, except for all those that fail to do so. That is why it is vital to understand not only that free speech is threatened, which it most certainly is, but also the very particular ways that free speech is under attack today, and not to let them go unchecked.

Whose freedom, whose speech

There is no single origin story for today's free speech controversies. But when it comes to US college campuses, which are crucibles for the wider society, one of the most prominent early altercations happened in 2015 at Yale University when a campus body known as the Intercultural Affairs Council sent an email to all students warning them against wearing 'culturally unaware and insensitive' Halloween costumes – including feathered

headdresses, and turbans – that could cause offence. In response, Erika Christakis, a child development expert and associate master of Yale's Silliman residential college, sent a message of her own to Silliman students. She argued that the directive infantilised the undergraduates, depriving them of agency to select their own costumes and deal with any fallout that might ensue with their peers. Christakis countered that the answer to potential offence over Halloween costumes was for those who might feel hurt to articulate and explain their feelings and for classmates accused of insensitivity to respond.

Christakis' email ignited a firestorm online and in the media after more than 740 students signed an open letter accusing her of riding roughshod over the sensitivities of historically underrepresented students, trivialising concerns over denigration, and validating expression that could erode their already precarious sense of belonging on campus. Christakis was prompted to resign.[6]

Days later the storm moved to the University of Missouri, where student protesters targeted campus leaders for failure to adequately address racism, forcing out the school's president and chancellor. A student photographer was manhandled while covering the demonstrations, with a media studies

professor, Melissa Click, calling for some 'muscle' to shove him away. The young journalist's entreaty, that 'the First Amendment protects your right to be here and mine', was ignored.

While the events at Yale and Missouri made national headlines, a set of wider trends was quietly taking hold. Pew Research Center reported that among eighteen- to twenty-nine-year-olds social media use had reached almost ninety per cent, reflecting a wholesale transformation in how young people were interacting and gleaning information.[7] A national poll published in October 2015 by the William F. Buckley Program at Yale reflected rising tensions between free speech and the imperative to avoid conflict and offence.[8] The survey reported nearly fifty per cent of students saying they sometimes or often felt intimidated and unable to share views that departed from those of classmates or professors. Seventy-two per cent said they thought their universities should be doing more to foster a diversity of opinions in the classroom and on campus. Seventy-two per cent also said they supported disciplining students or faculty who use 'language that is considered racist, sexist, homophobic or otherwise offensive'. At the same time, campuses reported mounting calls for 'trigger

warnings' on syllabi to notify students of potentially upsetting or objectionable material, disinvitations of speakers considered controversial, and calls for colleges to be maintained as psychologically 'safe spaces' where students could avoid being confronted by objectionable language or ideas.

The battle lines were drawn. On the left, activists had witnessed the power of online outrage and the media spotlight to take down those accused of complicity, indifference or ignorance in the face of racism or bigotry. More conservative constituencies were appalled at what they saw as left-wing intolerance. They labelled students claiming to be harmed by speech as 'snowflakes' who lacked resilience and were prone to demanding special treatment. They blamed such misguided sensibilities on a sense of learned frailty that they attributed in part to so-called 'helicopter parenting'. Erika Christakis' career-derailing email had cited a newly published article by psychologist Jonathan Haidt and free speech advocate Greg Lukianoff in *The Atlantic* magazine decrying what they called 'the coddling of the American mind', namely a misguided quest to 'scrub campuses clean of words, ideas, and subjects that might cause discomfort or give offense'. The trend, they argued, 'presumes an extraordinary fragility of the collegiate psyche'.[9]

Social media and viral videos of heated exchanges fed the fire. As I wrote at the time in a *New York Times* op-ed, 'all sides in this conflict are fast learning [that] the penalties of online pariahdom – damaged careers, vows of physical harm – can chill speech just as cold as the threat of jail'. I argued that free speech was a potent tool to protect and advance the rights of the disenfranchised, and equally, that proponents of 'safe spaces' risked suffocating themselves if they excluded contrarian views. I also pointed out that we must hear out a rising generation voicing genuine concerns about the unfinished business of the civil rights movement and the forging of a more equal society, and work to convince them that free speech could aid, rather than impede, those causes. Such pleas for a nuanced understanding of the merits and fallacies on both sides of the argument went largely unheeded as speech-related controversies multiplied.

Speech, hate and harm

In the same period, President Donald Trump took office. His calls for a visa ban on Muslims, derisive comments about Mexicans, and retweeting of

neo-Nazis during his 2016 campaign represented a harsh backlash against the racially progressive spirit that had propelled the rise of Barack Obama eight years earlier on a message of hope and change. Under Trump, forms of denigration that had become taboo in many circles were suddenly legitimised from the bully pulpit of the White House. Trump's comments after the deadly white supremacist rally in Charlottesville, Virginia in August 2017, that 'both sides' were to blame and that there were 'some very fine people' among those marauding with torches and racist chants, were read as a plain endorsement of biased and vitriolic speech and action.

Concerns that hateful speech was coursing freely through society with encouragement from the president fed an impulse by institutional leaders across the country to cordon off their establishments. University presidents, publishers, editors and businesspeople took what they saw as a moral stand to protect, within the domains under their control, members of vulnerable communities who felt menaced in Donald Trump's America. As Trump made the United States more hospitable to expressions of intolerance, guardians of smaller spheres – universities, corporations, organisations – felt duty

bound to counterbalance his influence through steps to safeguard their constituents not just physically, but psychologically. Starbucks founder Howard Schulz convened an emergency meeting of employees under the banner of 'Hate Has No Home Here'. Corporations including Google and Apple spoke out publicly to denounce the Charlottesville riot. Tech companies took steps to expunge extremist groups from their platforms.[10] Yard signs proclaiming 'Hate Has No Home Here' in multiple languages popped up on lawns. These were benevolent measures, and felt necessary to allay fears and signify that America would not devolve into a place where racial and ethnic hatred would be increasingly mainstreamed. By putting the dangers of speech on conspicuous display, Trump heralded a culture of more assertive patrolling of speech in the name of curbing its evident link to real world harms.

In a series of incidents on campuses, professors came under fire for uttering the n-word. They were not using it as a slur, but rather citing literary references from James Baldwin or Mark Twain or, in other cases, offering an example to illustrate a juridical doctrine in a law school class. When confronted, they insisted they were not 'using' the word, but rather just 'mentioning' it, a distinction

with well-established significance to scholars and linguists. But when it came to this singular slur, at a moment of heightened sensitivity to hateful speech, there was little patience for that subtlety. Students insisted that the offensive power of the word, no matter the intent or context in which it was being used, should render it out of bounds. Professors who had used the word in the course of classroom teaching for years suddenly found themselves subject to complaints and demands for discipline. Walter Mosley, a Black novelist and screenwriter, wrote of being called out of a Hollywood writers' room to the television studio's human resources department after a fellow writer complained about his use of the n-word in recounting a story about a cop. Mosley was so chagrined that he quit the gig, exclaiming that 'I *am* the N-word in the writers' room.'[11]

More expansive invocations of the language of harm in relation to objectionable speech began to blur the bounds between expression that might be offensive to someone, and that which should be judged intolerable by everyone. Students on some campuses stressed a point made in response to the Christakis memo, namely that even debating such distinctions and litigating the magnitude of alleged speech infractions posed a tangible burden

on students whose identity groups were implicated. By having to explain how speech landed, they were being forced into confrontational conversations, and required to bear the emotional and intellectual toll of having to educate ill-informed and sometimes dubious classmates or instructors. By declaring objectionable speech out of bounds, that onus could be lifted from the shoulders of those in vulnerable groups. Such calls were often well-intended efforts to rebalance a discourse that seemed to tilt in the direction of normalising hatred and insult.

But as I wrote in a 2018 *Washington Post* op-ed, 'campus protesters sometimes conflate truly threatening speech with ideas that, while discomforting, objectionable or even insulting to some, are precisely the sort of thing that ought to be aired and debated.[12] There are important differences between white-supremacist rallies and debates over affirmative action or the Israel–Palestine conflict.' But such distinctions were gradually being lost as even reasoned, academic discussions or online debates of hot button topics became fodder to discredit and ridicule proponents of disfavoured ideas. In September 2018 *New York Review of Books* editor Ian Buruma was forced from his job after just sixteen months due to the publication of an essay by a

Canadian journalist who argued, after being acquitted of sexual assault charges, that he was the victim of overzealousness by the #MeToo movement. The left-leaning *Review* staff leaked their outrage on social media, pressured *Review* advertisers and prompted the editor's ouster. Buruma explained that he had hoped the article would explore the complexities of alleged villains acquitted by courts but convicted on social media, only to become a victim of the online outrage machine himself.

Equity, inclusion and chill

As part of their effort to project their values more clearly in the face of Trump, many liberal institutions invested in diversity, equity and inclusion (DEI) programmes in order to better reflect the needs and participation of diverse constituencies including historically excluded racial groups, LGBTQ individuals, Muslim Americans and more. Newly created or expanded DEI offices were built out of the important recognition that simply bringing in more diverse cohorts of employees or students was not enough to transform workplaces or universities into places truly hospitable to, and

reflective of, a pluralistic population. DEI teams do essential work, including creating awareness of and sensitivity towards sometimes latent biases, elevating and celebrating diverse cultures, and supporting individuals to succeed notwithstanding financial, social or academic barriers.

In some instances, DEI administrators interpreted their mandate as involving placing restrictions on speech in the name of creating a more welcoming setting for those who might feel marginalised on the basis of their race, sexual orientation or gender identity. At some universities, new systems for reporting on incidents of bias – including through anonymous submissions – became an invitation for complaints over comments that were considered objectionable or unwelcome.[13] Some policies required every complaint to be investigated, regardless of whether the speech in question would have been widely considered offensive, whether it reflected any animus, or whether it provoked actual feelings of upset or victimisation for any specific individual. Privacy protections for complainants sometimes meant that those under investigation were not made aware of the precise charges against them, nor who had raised them. Probes could lead to discipline or even referrals to law enforcement.

Even if the expression in question was ultimately adjudicated as non-violating, the bias response inquiries themselves could subject students and faculty to prolonged investigations and cast a chill on the discussion of controversial topics.

As the bias response teams illustrated, an inherent dilemma in trying to contain the spread of offensive speech relates to where expressive boundaries should be drawn. In US tort law, for example, courts often apply a 'reasonable person standard' to assess whether a defendant exercised the degree of care that could be expected under the circumstances. A reasonable person is defined as one who applies an average level of care, caution and consideration when, for example, driving a car or taking a pit-bull for a walk. In theory, a similar standard might informally be applied to speech: whether words, phrases or slogans are ones that a reasonable person would know were considered offensive or likely to inflict psychological discomfort.

But when it comes to the use of language in a pluralistic society, there is no single reasonable person. Differences of background, upbringing, ethnicity, age, race, religion and other factors inflect the meaning of speech in ways that don't affect judgements over how to drive a car or walk a dog. What is offensive

to some is anodyne to others, and vice versa. The 2024 protests over the Israel–Hamas war have occasioned fierce debate over the meaning of slogans and whether they are appropriately considered offensive, hateful or even genocidal. In considering contested perspectives regarding offence, it is important to take account of the views of those who feel vulnerable as a result of particular speech. The views of young students of colour on the import of the Confederate flag should not be brushed aside, even in the face of arguments that it is a symbol of Southern pride or that it represents a link to family heritage. While the perspective of those who feel imperilled by words or symbols may not always win the day, it should not be dismissed. Particularly when members of a vulnerable group have made their interpretation of a word or slogan well known, as happened with the n-word in the course of multiple, well-publicised incidents, it is incumbent on speakers to take account of those views. They should not simply rest on the notion that they do not wilfully intend to offend or trigger through the use of terms that others have indicated will do just that.

On some campuses, faculty job candidates faced new requirements to proffer 'DEI statements' outlining their own commitment and experience in

fostering diversity in their prior academic posts. Such statements, in the view of PEN America and other free speech groups, impinge upon academic freedom by creating an ideological litmus test and imposing a requirement of 'compelled speech' that runs counter to the First Amendment and to private universities' commitments to academic freedom. The very fact of being asked to produce a DEI statement can be enough to suggest to a job candidate that certain positions, views and approaches towards diversity are expected, and will be considered a qualification for the job they seek. Knowing that, the submission of such a statement could become a rote exercise in parroting language that the candidate believes hiring committee members might want to hear. While there is merit in ensuring that prospective hires have an opportunity to highlight the contributions they are poised to make toward diversity and other institutional values, such emphasis should not be compelled. Amid such criticisms, in the spring of 2024 the Massachusetts Institute of Technology eliminated required diversity statements, declaring that: 'We can build an inclusive environment in many ways, but compelled statements impinge on freedom of expression, and they don't work.' Other universities were expected to follow suit.[14]

Battles between defenders and critics of DEI escalated to the point where some opponents began to argue for the elimination of DEI entirely, on the grounds that it had hardened into a rigid, speech-suppressive ideology. Such critiques tended to focus on high-profile incidents of overreach rather than reckoning with the breadth of DEI work and the crucial benefits it offers in fostering institutional self-reflection and for students and faculty in need of support. DEI efforts were caricatured as zealotry, rather than looked at objectively as a vital, expanding discipline that would continue to evolve, if imperfectly. Feeding into a larger backlash against progressive policies and ideas, legislators in certain states moved to defund and ban university DEI offices or otherwise hobble their work.

I have often been asked why free speech and issues of equity and inclusion seem so frequently to clash, and why now. The drive to rectify long-standing policies and structures predicated on biased and dated notions about race, gender, sexuality and other facets of identity is not new. In most realms of American society, formal equality – laws guaranteeing equality in employment, education, public places and other realms – has been in effect for decades. But disparities in wealth, education,

health and other measures persist, making plain that the lingering effects of racism and other forms of bigotry remain entrenched.

Tackling this deeper level of attitudes and biases – work that I have mentioned earlier as the unfinished business of the civil rights movement – necessarily requires that we re-examine not just laws and policies, but also how we think of and speak to each other. Understanding how a concept such as unconscious bias operates, for example, leads naturally to scrutiny and reappraisal of speech. We may use slurs, biased tropes or outdated terms about a group of people to whom we have had little exposure. We may repeat historical theories or interpretations that are predicated on dated conceptions of race that we were taught years ago and have not been prompted to rethink. We may ask questions or make gestures – moving to touch someone's hair, or complimenting an unfamiliar accent – that inadvertently reveal just how unfamiliar we are with someone from a different background, making them feel uncomfortable or as if their identity sets them apart from others.

These manifestations of racial perception and bias – and the conversations required to identify and deal with them – inevitably involve what we

should and should not say, why, and how those understandings are inculcated. The same is true in terms of reckoning with various other manifestations of bigotry, including misogyny and homophobia. We may judge women more harshly for failing to show empathy or vulnerability in situations where the same would not be expected of a man. We may make assumptions about a person's sexual orientation, or how it correlates with their style of dress or taste in entertainment. Such comments and references can make the vulnerable party feel denigrated and discriminated against. Preventing that from happening demands more attention to – and conscientiousness about – speech. If no one is willing to tell us that the term we have used is out-of-date or objectionable, we may not find out until it's too late to prevent an unintended offence or source of friction.

That today's debates over inclusion implicate speech is therefore understandable, unavoidable and necessary. In a pluralistic society, conscientiousness with language is less an inhibitor of expression than an enabler of it. Free speech is not simply the right to shout at the top of your lungs. We protect free speech not as an end unto itself, but because it is the foundation of our ability to

persuade, bond with, understand and connect with others. Philosophers, political theorists and jurists point to ways in which free speech and open discourse foster a healthier and more evolved society. They cite the value of free speech to expose ideas to scrutiny and reveal which competing claims have the virtue of truth; to enable arts, culture and creativity to flourish and to serve as a catalyst for scientific, technological and social progress; and to provide a vital safeguard and tool for the expression of individual identity.

If, while trying to get a point across, we inadvertently blunder into causing offence, our ability to convince others, win an argument, elucidate truth or deepen relationships is undercut. Slurs and denigrating speech stoke hostility and anxiety, eroding prospects for mutual understanding. The tension caused by errant language can detract from the topic at hand or antagonise an interlocutor, distracting from the ideas a speaker hoped to purvey. By contrast, conscientiousness – taking note of who is in your audience, staying up to speed on social norms, paying attention to inclusive language – can help smooth the path towards being heard. In that sense, sensitivity to bigotry is not at odds with the exercise of speech rights, but rather an enabler of

the end goals of speaking up – not just to sound off, but to be understood. A general norm of conscientiousness can make space for more contentious discussions. If people are relatively at home in a campus or work setting and feel their sensitivities are, by and large, respected, they will be less prone to take umbrage at a microaggression or the voicing of a viewpoint they find objectionable. By contrast, in a setting where offences are frequent, each one takes on increased weight as part of what may be an intolerable pattern. In an environment experienced as generally respectful there will be greater scope to enter into edgy conversations without fear of stoking outrage.

Cancelling each other out

During Trump's years in the White House, controversies over offensive speech continued to metastasise. In 2018 actress Rosanne Barr saw her television show, and her career, terminated within hours of posting a tweet that used the notorious racist trope of an ape to mock Valerie Jarrett, a top advisor to President Barack Obama. Blockbuster *Harry Potter* author J. K. Rowling came under fire for her views

on feminism and womanhood, which some saw as an affront to transgender identities.

The heightened vigilance targeting offensive speech also affected book publishing. Unwritten rules came to govern who had the authority to tell which stories, with acts of alleged literary trespass – intruding into a realm of storytelling where some believed a particular author did not belong – punished by opprobrium and cancellation. The most notorious case involved the 2020 publication of *American Dirt*, a much-heralded novel by Jeanine Cummins about a Mexican bookseller forced to flee across the border with her young son. Essayist Myriam Gurba, whose mother is Mexican, excoriated the book as 'appropriating genius works by people of color', and concluded that 'the nicest thing I can say about *Dirt* is that its pages ought to be upcycled as toilet paper'.[15] Cummins, who has one Puerto Rican grandmother, was vilified by some progressive writers who argued that her handsome advance and generous promotional budget should have gone to a writer with stronger Latino heritage.[16] Cummins herself anticipated the critique, writing that 'I wished someone slightly browner than me would write it.'

Some argued that the issue was not Cummins'

ethnicity but rather the poor quality of her novel. Writing in the *New York Times*, critic Parul Sehgal judged Cummins' book to read 'conspicuously like the work of an outsider', but also noted that its overriding 'failures . . . have little to do with the writer's identity and everything to do with her abilities as a novelist'.[17] But there is no single arbiter of taste and truth in literature. While Myriam Gurba loathed *American Dirt*, novelist Sandra Cisneros, the daughter of two Mexican parents and a celebrated pillar of the Chicano literary movement, blurbed it as 'the great novel of the Americas'. There is nothing wrong with sharp disagreement over the merits of a book. The notion that an author venturing into unfamiliar cultural terrain bears a higher burden to achieve accuracy and authenticity is not unfair; anyone who chooses to tackle an unfamiliar topic holds that obligation. But when a public attack is not limited to the substance of what has been written but also calls into question the author's right to even put such a story to paper, the reverberations go beyond that individual writer.

The attacks on Cummins, which led her publisher to cancel her book tour but did not prevent *American Dirt* from becoming a bestseller, were inflamed by longstanding frustrations at hurdles

faced by writers of colour pursuing literary careers. The controversy prompted a viral social media campaign under the hashtag #PublishingPaidMe which exposed racial disparities in compensation. The resulting uproar helped spark a concerted drive by major publishers to diversify the senior ranks of their editorial staff, open new imprints aimed at elevating writers of colour, and identify a wider array of literary talent.

PEN America wrote two reports on these subjects: the first, published in October 2022, was *Reading Between the Lines: Race, Equity, and Book Publishing*.[18] The study looked at factors – hiring patterns, bookselling methods, marketing strategies and more – that had slowed diversification in book authors and narratives over decades. A second report, *Booklash: Literary Freedom, Online Outrage and the Language of Harm*, examined how sometimes rigid notions of what should entitle an author to write a book, or disqualify them from doing so – whether their racial, ethnic or gender identity, past misdeeds, choice of subject matter or simply their perceived lack of skill or nuance as a writer handling sensitive topics – were leading publishing houses and writers themselves to pull back from risk-taking and even cancel the planned publication

of books out of fear of backlash.[19] Despite prompting the cancellation of her book tour, the *American Dirt* controversy did not ultimately hamper Jeanine Cummins' ability to purvey her story to readers. But, as the *Booklash* report recounted, 'the episode left many within the literary world with the impression that books perceived to trespass across racial or cultural lines could be risky and undesirable'. 'Certainly,' said a former editor, 'the *American Dirt* controversy brought up a lot around the idea of, "Are we saying that not anyone can write any story? Do you have to have a certain identity?" There's a lot of fear around that.'

When caution becomes chill

In a 2018 survey by the *New York Times*, a majority of students said that, while they valued both goals, creating a diverse and inclusive society was more important than protecting free speech.[20] College professors who tackled rape or transgender issues in the classroom had begun to face student complaints that could trigger prolonged and burdensome investigations. As Harvard law professor Jeannie Suk Gersen had first recounted in a 2014 *New Yorker*

article, about a dozen teachers of criminal law at other institutions had told her that they were not going to include rape law in their class, 'arguing that it's not worth the risk of complaints of discomfort by students'.[21]

By 2019 Lukianoff and Haidt, who had turned their *Atlantic* article on the coddling of the American mind into a book, were warning of professors 'teaching on tenterhooks' or 'walking on eggshells' in the classroom. A 2019 survey by College Pulse reported majorities of students saying that it was at least sometimes acceptable to shout down campus speakers or otherwise prevent them from speaking. As the drive to cancel, suppress and punish speech spread, it began to elicit a stronger backlash.[22] In an October 2019 interview, former President Barack Obama criticised the prevailing 'call-out culture' and 'wokeness', urging young activists to recognise that 'the world is messy; there are ambiguities', and that 'people who do really good stuff have flaws'.

The strains intensified further in 2020. The May murder by Minneapolis police of an unarmed Black man, George Floyd, turbocharged a national movement to accelerate racial justice and dismantle institutions and systems judged to perpetuate

racial bias and inequities. The mantra of 'Black Lives Matter' was broadly embraced, with institutions of all stripes issuing statements and pledges to eradicate racism in their ranks. A series of high-profile incidents underscored that reprisals for speech that defied prevailing sentiments on issues of racial justice could be unforgiving. *New York Times* editorial page editor James Bennet was forced out for greenlighting an op-ed by Arkansas Senator Tom Cotton arguing that the National Guard should be called in to quell unruly protests. Some of the newspaper's staffers claimed not just that the piece was objectionable but that it could put them in danger, presumably by legitimising the use of force to quell protests they were covering in the course of their work. While the newspaper's leaders initially pledged to stand by the controversial inflammatory op-ed as presenting a reasoned viewpoint by an influential senator, they quickly succumbed to staff fury. Though they said the retraction was motivated by factual errors and lapses in the vetting process, those claims were later debunked.

That incident – where the protest came from inside the house – exerted a uniquely potent chilling effect. It underscored that even within the staff of

the *Times*, the notion of an editorial page giving voice to a wide range of views – including those some might find odious – was no longer broadly accepted. The assertion that ideas could cause harm or danger to vulnerable people carried such weight that any attempt to question or argue back could be cast as indifferent, reckless or racist. The interplay of speech and harm became a defining characteristic of free speech debates, with claims of harm emboldening calls to suppress and punish speech in the name of safeguarding against tangible and lasting ills.

Many free speech defenders are reluctant to acknowledge that speech can cause harm for fear that doing so is an invitation to censorship. I have argued that a persuasive defence of speech allows that such harms are real. Psychological studies show that individuals subjected to pervasive stereotyping, slurs or denigration throughout their lives can manifest the emotional and even physical toll of such affronts. Those consequences should be recognised and are a reason to intensify efforts to combat racism and other forms of denigration. They are also a reason that retiring dated terms that may have once been commonplace but have come to be seen as dated or denigrating should not be considered an affront to free speech; updating language conventions to better

reflect an evolving society can help ensure that the widest segment of the population has a voice. But it is also true that the claimed harms of speech can be exaggerated, projected or imagined. Just because something might be construed as offensive doesn't mean anyone was actually offended, much less harmed. Fleeting feelings of hurt or upset are not the same as lasting harms. The language of harm in relation to speech must be used sparingly and with care. Where such claims of harm are thrown around loosely, they can give rise to both formal repression of speech and a tacit awareness that bold, unfiltered expression may carry too much risk.

The move to expunge objectionable sentiments reverberated through the wider culture. In June 2020 HBO announced that it would purge *Gone With the Wind* from its streaming service because it glorified the antebellum South. The network reversed its decision after being reminded that the film had boasted the first Black recipient of an Oscar and remained a valued text for understanding the period. Thereafter the film was introduced with a message offering historical context. In September 2020 the Burbank Unified School District in Los Angeles voted to ban all books containing the n-word, taking treasured novels

including *Huckleberry Finn* and *Roll of Thunder, Hear My Cry* off shelves.[23]

Feeling the space for intellectual expression constrict around them, in July 2020 a group of 152 centrist, liberal and left-wing scholars and authors including Salman Rushdie, Reginald Dwayne Betts, Margaret Atwood, Atul Gawande, Wynton Marsalis, Cornel West, Francis Fukuyama and Noam Chomsky issued a joint letter published in *Harper's* magazine which called out the 'intolerance of opposing views, a vogue for public shaming and ostracism, and the tendency to dissolve complex policy issues in a blinding moral certainty', which they witnessed among both left and right.[24] The writers decried the way that 'editors are fired for running controversial pieces; books are withdrawn for alleged inauthenticity; journalists are barred from writing on certain topics; professors are investigated for quoting works of literature in class; a researcher is fired for circulating a peer-reviewed academic study; and the heads of organizations are ousted for what are sometimes just clumsy mistakes. Whatever the arguments around each particular incident, the result has been to steadily narrow the boundaries of what can be said without the threat of reprisal.'

The backlash against the letter was fierce.

Coming amid Black Lives Matter protests, it was seen by some as a distraction and by others as an attempt by privileged academics and thinkers to curtail the power of a rising flank of the previously marginalised who were enjoying newfound – and overdue – public influence. It spurred a counter-letter signed by 160 other academics and journalists, some of whom remained anonymous, arguing that: 'Under the guise of free speech and free exchange of ideas, the letter appears to be asking for unrestricted freedom to espouse their points of view free from consequence or criticism . . . they have no intention of sharing that space or acknowledging their role in perpetuating a culture of fear and silence among writers who, for the most part, do not look like the majority of the signatories.'[25] Some critics excoriated the original letter not based on its content, but because the signatories included intellectuals with varied views on hot button issues including trans-gender rights. The implicit notion was that in order to make common cause on anything with anyone, one had to agree with them on every issue of consequence. Signatory Malcolm Gladwell tweeted that he 'signed the Harpers [sic] letter because there were lots of people who also signed the Harpers letter whose views I disagreed with. I thought that was

the point of the Harpers letter.' The *Harper's* letter debate put a spotlight on the constraints and inhibitors of open discourse. It provided cover in certain circles for those wishing to speak out and take risks, while also underscoring the perils of doing so.

Soft censoriousness meets hard censorship

While centre and centre-left thinkers were protesting the rise of censoriousness through an appeal to liberal values, conservative American politicians were beginning to mobilise more coercive means. Alongside greater awareness of race, gender and other forms of diversity came a wider reckoning with the place of identity in US history and society. Persistent manifestations of racism prompted journalists, scholars and educators to examine the unique role of race in America. The 1619 Project, an essay series published by the *New York Times Magazine* in 2019, argued that the year that slaves first arrived in Virginia was a more fitting starting point for explorations of American history than the traditional focus on 1776 as the year the United States was founded. The project, which yielded a Pulitzer Prize for *Times*

journalist Nikole Hannah-Jones, sparked vigorous debate both as a matter of history and as a reframing of national lore. Many considered the 1619 Project an empowering rebuke to national narratives seen to glorify leaders, philosophies and institutions that systematically excluded and repressed Black Americans. Critics, on the other hand, included distinguished historians who pointed out interpretive inaccuracies in the work. The project also had detractors who were less focused on historical accuracy than on interpretation; they rejected the project's themes as an affront to national pride and patriotism, including faith in the Founding Fathers and Constitution. The 1619 Project inspired educators to rethink the teaching of history and was adapted into a curriculum for schools and higher education. Its influence, in turn, sparked fears from the right that students would now be presented a version of US history that they saw as distorted and misleading.

Amid this fast-changing national conversation on issues of race came intensified attention on questions of gender. Within a relatively short space of time after the Supreme Court offered national legal recognition of gay marriage in 2015, transgender, non-binary and gender-fluid identities came to be more widely adopted and openly discussed. DEI offices reinforced

the importance of calling individuals by their preferred pronouns. Corporations and institutions took steps to reflect greater gender diversity with respect to bathrooms, sports teams, styles of dress and other societal norms and structures. Publishers began to seek out and elevate books encompassing a wider array of authors, and addressing topics such as race and gender, including for children and young adults.

The reshaping of historical and social narratives was seen by many on the left as a vital, valiant corrective necessary to realise the promise of an inclusive society. Others, on the right, regarded the emergence of such educational materials as an intrusive, heretical effort to impose newfangled values. Many or most Americans probably fall somewhere in between, wanting broad access to books and a variety of perspectives that allow students and citizens to draw their own conclusions. The tension between these values and priorities would intensify and become a primary driver of outright censorship in the United States.

Mostly spontaneous, organic efforts to police speech through social stigma and shifting norms were then met with systematic efforts to use legislation and formal bans to fence off controversial narratives and ideas. The language of harm,

invoked by some on the left as grounds to demand censure for speech, was appropriated by the right as grounds to declare progressive books and ideas dangerous. In a 2018 speech, US Attorney General Jeff Sessions lambasted incursions on speech by the 'hard left', stoking an audience composed of conservative students to fight against 'elements in our society today who want to stop you and silence you'. In March 2019, at the Conservative Political Action Conference, President Trump announced plans for an executive order that would link federal research funding to institutions agreeing to promote 'free inquiry'. He professed to be taking 'historic action to defend American students and American values that have been under siege'. While benign and even speech-affirming on its face, the measure was seen by many higher education leaders as an opening salvo intended to strike fear among tertiary education administrators that the federal government – a source of billions in funding for research and financial aid even at private universities – was watching closely how universities were handling political debates and treating conservative students.

Over the twelve months beginning in January 2021, 156 bills were introduced or pre-filed in

thirty-nine states that met PEN America's definition of an 'educational gag order': namely a state
legislative or policy effort to restrict teaching and
learning in educational settings.[26] The measures
addressed topics including race, gender, American
history and LGBTQ identities, restricting and
mandating whether and how they were taught and
discussed in schools and, in some cases, higher education. The most notorious among these included
Florida's House Bill 1557 of 2022, known colloqui-
ally in some circles as the state's 'Don't Say Gay' law.
The measure's stated purpose was to 'prohibit classroom discussion about sexual orientation or gender
identity in certain grade levels or in a specified
manner'. Proponents of the law maintained that
this was its sole purpose, to ensure that sex education was age appropriate. A Florida Department of
Education directive implementing the law banned
in-class teaching of content relating to sexual orientation and gender identity for students aged five
to eighteen, with few exceptions. Soon after Florida's law was enacted, legislators in a dozen other
states took steps to follow suit. In March 2024 the
state of Florida settled a suit by civil rights attor-
neys challenging H.B. 1557 by agreeing that while
gender 'ideology' would continue to be barred from

classroom instruction, the prohibition would not apply to less formal references to LGBTQ identity in books or in class discussions.

Rising up against the perceived imposition of left-wing orthodoxies in public education, conservative countermeasures have also included targeted campaigns to ban books, many linked to subject-matter-based legislative prohibitions. As of December 2023, PEN America had documented over 6,000 book bans in public schools, affecting 247 school districts in forty-one states.[27] The bans overwhelmingly affect books by and about people of colour and LGBTQ individuals. The bans have swept up the works of bestselling authors including Jodi Picoult, Laurie Halse Anderson and Rupi Kaur, among others, as well as classic works including Art Spiegelman's graphic novel *Maus*, *The Diary of Anne Frank*, Toni Morrison's *Beloved* and John Steinbeck's *Of Mice and Men*. The grounds for withholding the books can include isolated discussions or depictions of sex that are mischaracterised as pornographic or obscene, violence or offensive language, themes involving race or gender, disputed historical events or just about anything that someone, somewhere finds objectionable. Novelist Ann Patchett quipped that her book *The Patron Saint of Liars*, which is

set in a home for unwed mothers, was banned in Orange County, Florida because the characters must have had sex in order to wind up as part of the story.

Conservative activist Chris Rufo has been explicit in using supposed liberal overreach in policing speech to justify his campaign to champion heavy-handed government intervention in the form of book bans and gag orders. In 2021 Rufo used the 1619 Project curriculum as a basis to argue that schoolchildren were being indoctrinated in 'critical race theory', a school of thought developed by left-wing legal scholars to draw attention to the role of race in shaping wide-ranging facets of American society. Rufo was open about seeking to 'put all of the various cultural insanities under that brand category' and 'to have the public read something crazy in the newspaper and immediately think "critical race theory"'. Another primary line of attack for Rufo is the contention that LGBTQ content is being promoted by educators at the risk of turning schools into 'hunting grounds for sexual predators', an outlandish contention that critics have decried as slanderous.

These developments have conspired to cast a chill over public education. In Florida, not one of

the forty presidents at public colleges and universities was willing to speak out against a proposed 2023 package of legislative reforms to ban DEI, weaken tenure protections and prohibit certain majors dealing with race and gender. The proposed measures were widely protested by national academic and scholarly associations, but Florida's own top higher education leaders remained mum. An analysis by Inside Higher Ed attributed the silence to fear, both for the leaders' own jobs and of the reprisals that might affect their institutions. The bill was somewhat weakened by the Florida Senate, but passed.

Calling a crisis a crisis

At this point, at least in the United States, denial that there exists a free speech crisis seems to be ebbing. The evidence is hard to ignore. In FIRE's 2023 campus free speech survey, as many as seventy-two per cent of student respondents registered opposition to allowing a conservative speaker on campus, depending on the topic; up to forty-three per cent of students were against allowing a liberal speaker on campus.[28] Hank Reichman, former chair

of the American Association of University Professors' Committee on Academic Freedom and Tenure, commented in early 2023 that academic freedom was 'more endangered now than at any time since the early 20th century'.

While they may disagree on the nature of the crisis, leading figures on both the right and the left in US politics and culture agree that free speech is in jeopardy. A May 2024 survey by FIRE found that two-thirds of Americans polled were 'concerned about the direction freedom of speech is heading in this country . . . regardless of which major candidate wins the 2024 presidential election'.[29] The survey revealed that fears with respect to the sanctity of First Amendment rights were most acute among conservative and very conservative Americans. But fears are also rising on the left and in the centre. In introducing a bill to combat book bans and protect educators in December 2023, liberal Democratic Congressman Jamie Raskin said: 'America is in the middle of an escalating book ban crisis that requires our full attention and a strong response. Sinister campaigns to remove books from our schools and libraries are a hallmark of authoritarian and fascist regimes.' Salman Rushdie, himself the victim of a 1989 fatwa by the Ayatollah of Iran

and, thirty-four years later, a knife attack on stage at a literary event in upstate New York, remarked in 2023 that 'freedom to publish has not in my lifetime been under such threat in the countries of the West'. The *New York Times* editorial board proclaimed in 2022 that 'America has a Free Speech Problem'. The board decried 'cancel culture', citing survey data showing that Americans 'both know it exists and feel its burden', as well as 'an avalanche of legislation passed by Republican-controlled legislatures around the country that gags discussion of certain topics and clearly violates the spirit of the First Amendment, if not the letter of the law'.[30]

Those who feel implicated in the crisis, or responsible for addressing it, are mobilising. In August 2023 a group of thirteen college presidents, including those of Cornell and Rutgers universities, joined the Campus Call for Free Speech, pledging to entrench free speech education and protections more firmly at their schools. Over 200 former college presidents and provosts have joined PEN America's Champions of Higher Education, pledging to safeguard higher education 'as an essential guarantor of free expression in a democracy' and to rally support against censorious legislation. Groups of faculty on dozens of campuses

have united in alliances to speak out on academic freedom.

Critics have questioned certain efforts to mobilise on behalf of academic freedom, charging their leaders with a self-serving approach that invokes free speech to reinforce the prerogatives of those with privilege and power. A *Harvard Crimson* editorial published in May 2023 in response to the formation of that school's academic freedom council criticised the group for seeming to dismiss student protesters and activists as agitators.[31] Though affirming their commitment to academic freedom, the student editorialists questioned whether the council's proponents were conflating free speech 'with freedom from criticism or accountability'. The editorial went on to single out several members of the council for writings or deeds that it judged 'flagrantly false', lacking in objectivity, or undermining of student trust, suggesting that such expression and actions were undeserving of protection. The piece insisted that '[t]hese improper actions cannot hide under calls to some "get out of jail free card" of academic freedom'. Those they challenged included Harvard Law School professor Mark Ramseyer, whose revisionist analysis of the terms upon which Korean

comfort women, long thought of as sex slaves, engaged with Japanese soldiers during the Second World War had occasioned a furious controversy among scholars. The editorial also charged law professor Ronald Sullivan with having 'betrayed the trust' of students in the undergraduate residential college he had headed because he served as part of the legal defence team in disgraced film mogul Harvey Weinstein's sexual assault trial. Though the student authors professed to recognise that academic freedom protects unpopular and contested expression, their call to delineate some positions as out of bounds seemed to validate faculty concerns that academic freedom was poorly understood and vulnerable to sacrifice in the name of other priorities.

Those who question whether free speech is under threat often do not actually contest that expression is being deterred and penalised. Rather, they maintain that such chilling can be a necessary corrective in a society marked by hateful rhetoric, political power imbalances, marginalisation and other social ills. Their claim, in essence, is that when addressing the societal problems they regard as uppermost seems incompatible with a robust regime of free speech, sacrificing the latter for the

former can be a worthy trade-off. That is a valid case to make, but it is less an argument that free speech is not under threat than an argument that free speech being under threat ought not trouble us too much. The point also fails to address the problem of threats to free speech, including book bans, legislative prohibitions and restrictions on protest, that target the very books, curricula or campaigns that elevate lesser-heard voices and narratives and counteract inequities. In the United States, those forces have helped a wider constituency, including on the progressive left, appreciate that they have a stake in free expression, and that free speech rights are essential to safeguarding the vulnerable as much as – if not more than – the powerful.

Combat hate, not speech

One reason some analysts are reluctant to acknowledge the threat to free speech is fear that such a position readily bleeds into the defence of hateful and harmful speech. Some of that hesitation is grounded in genuine concern about noxious speech and its impact. It can also be motivated by worry that defending free speech risks being misconstrued

as legitimising – or even just turning a blind eye towards – bigotry and abuse. The key to shoring up broad-based support for free speech is recognising that there is no contradiction between acknowledging the problems of hateful and offensive speech as a source of strife, discrimination and even violence in society *and* believing that free speech is widely threatened and deserves better protection from attack on all sides. These ideas should not be pitted against each other. The PEN International Charter, first drafted in 1948, commits the organisation to efforts to 'dispel all hatreds' and to oppose 'any form of suppression of freedom of expression'.[32] Writing in the wake of the Second World War, the charter's European drafters recognised that in the aftermath of the Holocaust no credible campaign for free speech could be silent about bigotry. That prescient insight informs PEN America's work. The charter is a charge both to take seriously the dangers of degrading and menacing speech, and to combat them through means that protect the maximum scope of expressive rights. Seventy-five years after its drafting, navigating the interplay of bigotry, inclusion and free speech in a diverse pluralistic democracy has become even more fraught, and even more essential.

Both US and international law offer important guidance on how to uphold free speech rights without allowing bigotry free rein. Even under the US First Amendment, certain forms of hateful and offensive speech can be banned and prosecuted consistent with the Constitution. When speech amounts to harassment of an individual, creates a hostile workplace or educational environment, constitutes a credible threat or incites imminent violence, it can be prohibited notwithstanding the First Amendment. Under international law the carve-outs are larger, allowing governments to ban speech that constitutes incitement to hatred or discrimination, categories that are less precise and allow for broader restrictions on, for example, Holocaust denial or blasphemy. In the United States in recent years, there have been several prominent examples of offensive falsehoods forming the basis for successful defamation lawsuits yielding vast monetary judgements. These include a suit filed against radio talk show host Alex Jones by parents of child victims of a school shooting in Sandy Hook, Connecticut. Jones was found to have wilfully inflicted emotional distress on the devastated families by denying that the attack took place and accusing them of being 'crisis actors'. After declining to contest the families'

claims in court, Jones was slapped with a billion-dollar damage award for defamation. Other major successful defamation suits include Dominion Voting Systems' $787.5 million settlement with Fox News over false charges that the company's machines thwarted the results of the 2020 election, and writer E. Jean Carroll's $83.3 million verdict against Donald Trump for baselessly claiming Carroll had lied in accusing him of assault. These judgements were rendered consistent with First Amendment free speech protections, which make exceptions for defamation and libel.

While some free speech experts have cautioned that these eye-popping verdicts could cast a chill over journalists, newsrooms or politicians, they may stand to have speech-protective effects. For one thing, the accusations and evidence against these perpetrators were explosive and extreme; it's hard to envision a mainstream journalist or public official being charged with comparable acts of knowing and persistent propagation of provably defamatory falsehoods. These high-profile verdicts may also play a role in buttressing faith in the existing US legal regimes governing speech. Those arguing for stiffer restrictions on expression maintain that traditional conceptions of the limited

role of government in policing speech are relics of a bygone era of pamphlets and printing presses, when the harms of speech were far more easily contained. In light of these shifts, the argument goes, our faith in the First Amendment, ratified 233 years ago, is now misplaced and must give way to more stringent, government-enforced limits on speech. The use of existing legal precedents and doctrines – such as defamation – to rein in some of the most egregious forms of expression can help blunt such calls to pare back speech protections. When people witness Alex Jones' media empire and Fox News being held accountable in monetary terms that bite, the outcomes can shore up public confidence that, at least with respect to certain very harmful forms of content, our existing system does offer recourse. That, in turn, can help temper calls for new and more restrictive laws governing speech.

Other exceptions to the First Amendment – for harassment, incitement to imminent violence, and true threats (defined as expressions of serious intent to commit an act of violence against a group or individual) – also provide a basis for using existing law to combat offensive speech. Depending upon the circumstances, some of the most potent forms of offence, including racial and ethnic slurs

or calls for violence, can meet the legal definition of harassment, making them legally punishable. Outside the United States, where free speech protections are somewhat looser, bigoted speech may be actionable as incitement to hatred or as discrimination. In the United Kingdom, defamation law traditionally did not require that a plaintiff prove that a besmirching claim was false, but rather put the onus on the defendant to substantiate that the allegedly defamatory contention was true. That lower burden on defamation plaintiffs made British jurisdictions an appealing venue for libel claims, prompting the adoption of the 2013 Defamation Act which narrowed the criteria for a successful claim.

The First Amendment also allows for 'time, place and manner' restrictions governing things like when and where protests can be mounted and whether amplification can be used. Under some circumstances, these can help protect against menacing speech. In the US campus controversies of late 2023 and 2024, rowdy, persistent demonstrations fed claims that certain campuses had become hostile environments for Jewish, Israeli, Muslim or Arab students. 'Hostile environment' is a statutory term that reflects the failure of an institution to adequately protect individuals against

harassment. Students complained of being confronted by protests involving incendiary chants in libraries or outside lecture halls during exam periods or of being blocked from accessing parts of the campus based on their identity or viewpoint. In response, some universities stiffened their time, place and manner rules, for example prohibiting noisy protests indoors or in buildings where classes were in session. As long as the restrictions are reasonable and do not excessively curtail opportunities to assemble and be heard, such rules can expand the scope for speech that some may consider noxious by tamping down opposition and tempering demands to shut it down entirely. By enforcing reasonable time, place and manner rules, campuses can enable those who wish to avoid encountering protests that may involve denigrating slogans or motifs to know when and where such demonstrations may take place and to sidestep them. Such rules can thus protect against the impact of potentially hateful speech without shutting the speech down. The key to time, place and manner rules is that they must be reasonable, viewpoint-neutral, and applied evenhandedly whether the protest in question is to save the whales or decry religious extremism. The US has witnessed a pattern whereby particular protest

movements – be it the Black Lives Matter demonstrations in 2020 or the pro-Palestine campus encampments of 2024 – have spurred state legislators or college administrators to consider more stringent restrictions on assembly. Even if the regulations they propose are neutral on their face, the context in which they are put forward raises questions about legislative attempts to clamp down on speech on the basis of its content. Similar concerns have been raised in the UK over a new government definition of extremism which critics charge with being a thinly veiled attempt to curtail pro-Palestinian expression.

That offensive speech may not be grounds for prohibition or punishment does not mean that it should be tolerated, condoned or ignored. In the autumn of 2023, rhetoric on US college campuses heated up owing to the Israel–Hamas conflict. Most of the sloganeering and chants fell within the bounds of the First Amendment, but there were clear exceptions. At Cornell University a student posted online threats to kill and injure Jewish students, and ultimately pleaded guilty to federal charges carrying up to a five-year jail sentence. A leader in the protest movement at Columbia University stated in a video that 'Zionists don't deserve

to live' and that, in fighting a Zionist, 'I fight to kill'. Campuses have also witnessed cases of Islamophobia, including taunts, epithets, spitting and incidents that cross over from free speech to constituting potential hate crimes. These raised questions of how to respond to rising antisemitic and Islamophobic rhetoric and actions while upholding a campus commitment to allowing free speech.

Those unsettled and intimidated by hateful sentiments can be quick to demand that the noxious speech be suppressed through prohibition and punishment. They seek stiffened official restrictions and more assertive policing of speech as the most obvious route to rein in what offends and disturbs them. But there are good reasons why we limit the discretion of those in positions of authority to ban and punish speech, including speech we abhor.

First Amendment protections are in place because it is recognised that where officials have the leeway to police speech at will, they tend to abuse that authority in self-serving ways to clamp down on dissent, punish critics, safeguard their reputations, and silence voices they see as threatening to their status and rule. That is what authoritarian rulers in places like China, Russia and Iran do, sharply restricting speech that challenges their

preferred narratives and their grip on power. These authoritarians typically silence their critics by charging them with incitement, support for terrorism, sedition, or disruption to public order. In the absence of robust protections for free speech, these categories of errant speech can be expanded based on the whims of rulers to outlaw virtually anything they would rather not hear or read. Even in liberal-minded settings, when calls mount to patrol speech, the risk of overreach is real. In recent months, for example, campuses that came under fire for not doing enough to combat antisemitism have since gone to extremes involving speech suppression. In the case of the University of Indiana, a lawmaker had sent a letter to the institution threatening that if it failed to deal adequately with antisemitism, it could lose its federal funding. Soon thereafter the campus cancelled a long-planned exhibition of abstract paintings by an eighty-nine-year-old Palestinian-American artist, abstract paintings that were in no way alleged to bear antisemitic content.[33]

The aggressive policing of speech almost inevitably opens the door towards discrimination against particular opinions and ideologies. Under the First Amendment, permissible government restrictions on free speech must be viewpoint-neutral, applying

equally whether the speech in question is for or against the party in power, a war being fought, or a given political candidate. But human nature dictates that our own experiences, attitudes and predispositions inform how we exercise the authority we wield. One parent may harshly punish a child for using a curse word in frustration; another might forgive that infraction but clamp down on a kid for being rude to their grandmother. One of the most persistent critiques amid recent campus speech controversies is the charge of a double standard. The claim is that whereas universities became more aggressive in tamping down hateful expression during the Trump years and after the killing of George Floyd, similarly firm approaches have not been applied consistently. NYU professor Scott Galloway encapsulated a rising concern among some Jewish constituencies that 'free speech is at its freest when it is hate speech against Jews'. The allegations have not been limited to one side. After Columbia University's president testified before Congress and conveyed determined resolve to crack down on antisemitism, she was accused of pandering to wealthy donors and casting aside norms of academic freedom at the expense of pro-Palestinian expression.

Though hypocrisy in the name of free speech

is nothing new (and was described powerfully in Nat Hentoff's 1992 book, aptly titled *Free Speech for Me – But Not for Thee*), self-serving invocations of free speech point to a decay in understanding and appreciation of free speech as a norm and value that sits above politics and ideology. As left-leaning protesters come to realise the importance of free speech protections to the campaigns they are waging, the hope is that they will be awakened to the importance of supporting free speech as a principle, even for expression with which they disagree. At the same time, conservative proponents of book bans and prohibitions on curricula must recognise that by invoking the power of the state to ban and punish speech on the basis of the contents of a book or the ideas contained in a lesson, they are setting a precedent that could equally enable the extirpation of their own narratives and opinions.

Refusing to clamp down on hateful speech through bans and reprisals need not – and indeed must not – mean turning a blind eye to the impact of noxious speech. University leaders and others in positions of authority should respond forcefully to hateful speech through measures including counterspeech; the enforcement of reasonable neutral time, place and manner rules; gestures of

solidarity towards targeted groups; enhancements of physical security to ensure malign speech cannot cross over into violence; education to elucidate the impact of speech; dialogue that models reasoned disagreement; and related strategies. Such measures to address the impact of uncomfortable or intimidating speech can blunt calls to ban and punish expression. If those targeted by vituperation feel supported, protected and heard by those in authority, they will be better placed to withstand hostility from other quarters. Hateful speech is most potent where those victimised by it feel as if the sentiments expressed are not just those of the speaker, but are endorsed or condoned more broadly. The sense that hateful attitudes are widespread, and that those in positions of authority have failed to step in, can lead to feelings of deep vulnerability that manifest in outraged insistence that free speech safeguards be swept away in the name of safety.

The free speech crisis in context

While debates over campus culture and cancellation strike powerful chords in our public debate, they must not distract from a broader understanding

of the array of threats to free speech and open discourse, and the imperative of countering them. Any assessment of whether free speech is under threat must account for forces that impinge not just on the ability of individuals to voice their views, but on the benefits that open expression enables for a free society writ large. State-sponsored and particularly legislatively enshrined restrictions on free speech and open discourse represent a potent and durable threat that should rise to the top of the priority list for any defender of free expression. We must recognise the broad sweep of state censorship in schools in the US for what it is: an assault on specific identities, lifestyles, historical perspectives and ideas. By empowering individual citizens and parents to lodge complaints about specific books, which can prompt the removal of volumes from entire school systems serving tens of thousands of children for the duration of lengthy review processes, these laws allow the predilections of the few to override the rights of many.

At the same time, we must also recognise that racial, religious, cultural and socio-economic barriers can inhibit and impair self-expression, denying particular populations the full benefit of expressive rights. When individuals or groups are

excluded from participation as a result of lack of education or opportunities, the marketplace of ideas is impoverished and the quality of public discourse is compromised. Those who believe in free speech must tackle these boundaries as well. Such efforts should include steps to lower hurdles to accessing higher education and careers in journalism, writing, the arts and publishing so that these fields become more representative. Such measures are a boon to free expression by increasing the bounty of available perspectives and thereby helping accelerate the quest for truth as more ideas are tested against one another. Communities that have a voice in society will also be more invested in free speech as a principle, recognising that they too share in its dividends.

Some of the most potent threats to free speech and open discourse in the democratic world germinate online. In 2018 PEN America surveyed authors and journalists about online harassment, learning that trolling and digital aggression were forcing writers offline and interfering with their ability to reach readers, carry out research and engage in public debates.[34] Online abuse is overwhelmingly directed at women, LGBTQ individuals, people of colour, and members of historically

excluded racial and religious groups. Abusers zero in on those who venture to debate certain heated topics, such as sexual abuse, abortion or questions of gender identity. Preserving open access to digital discourse, including for those disproportionately targeted by abuse, has become a vital component of the defence of free expression.

Disinformation, fake news and manipulated media have the power to undermine public faith in the truth, yielding a polity in which citizens no longer know what to believe. We know from authoritarian regimes that where people despair of distinguishing fact from falsehood, they lose agency and tune out of civic life. This helps to explain why, for example, Russia's Vladimir Putin can claim overwhelming support in national elections. His opponents have been murdered, jailed or forced into exile; independent media have been shuttered; writers, artists, journalists and activists are persecuted; and those who remain see few avenues to effect change. For people living in an information ecosystem hopelessly polluted by disinformation, free speech loses much of its value. The fruits of free speech – including the ability to persuade, make common cause, press for social change and uncover truths – are out of reach where distrust

dominates and no one is sure what to believe. In a term later amplified by former President Barack Obama, journalism leader Sonni Efron has dubbed this phenomenon 'truth decay', citing the spread of conspiracy theories and deepening polarisation. Algorithmically enabled, engagement-based social media platforms pose a further threat to public discourse by funnelling users towards only the content they crave. Such platforms feed an information environment where people living in the same city and working in the same office may inhabit entirely different information ecosystems, disbelieving what they hear from one another

This mounting crisis in our shared information ecosystem is compounded by drastic shifts in how news is gathered, reported and consumed. The loss of the advertising revenue that long underwrote print newspapers has contributed to the erosion of civic trust and democratic accountability in many parts of the world. Surveys consistently show that local news is more trusted than any other source of journalism; yet local media outlets worldwide are struggling to survive. UN Secretary-General António Guterres warned in 2021 of 'a media extinction event' after news organisations reported near-fatal financial losses. As trusted news has

disappeared, disinformation has filled the void, with AI chatbots, propaganda sites and other spurious purveyors of information taking over where fact-checkers, journalists, editors and publishers once reigned. While the erosion of local news and the mounting spread of disinformation do not directly threaten the ability of citizens to speak out as they see fit, they accelerate declining trust in information and debate, undercutting the value of free speech as a catalyst for persuasion and understanding. In that sense, even though most disinformation would be protected by the First Amendment and international legal guardrails for free expression, the mire wrought by the spread of disinformation is also a compounding crisis for free speech.

Arguments against free speech

Some critics contend that the defence of free speech is little more than a licence to offend. Free speech has been derided as a weapon to deal blows to those in positions of precariousness. At times, though, the tables turn. Protesters aligned with the Palestinian cause have seen their speech suppressed and punished, but have also mounted demonstrations

so potent that they have prompted others to argue that their exercise of speech rights is overpowering campuses and subjecting fellow students to bigotry and ostracisation. The roles have reversed in that the left-leaning students and faculty who not long ago sometimes questioned the exercise of free speech rights in ways that could be offensive or unnerving to historically marginalised groups, may now be the ones asserting the right to disrupt and unsettle. Some more centrist or conservative voices accustomed to championing the exercise of speech rights to challenge left-wing orthodoxies are now revisiting their support for untrammelled free speech, arguing that if tacit or overt limits on speech exist to protect one marginalised group, they must apply equally to all, even if the net result is less speech and less freedom.

Free speech is not a licence to say anything to anyone for any reason. Nor is it a shield from the ramifications of words and ideas. We all recognise that if the consequences of speech are unbounded, the freedom to speak ceases to exist. When such consequences include jail, torture or extra-judicial killing, no one would argue that they are compatible with freedom. But when reprisals take the form of rebuttals, call-outs, ridicule, embarrassment,

harsh opprobrium, shunning or the loss of future speaking opportunities, these generally represent the protected expression of other speakers. Such responsive expression is not only legally protected, but also recognised as the rightful and best antidote to poisonous speech. As US Supreme Court Justice Louis Brandeis once famously proclaimed, the oft-touted best solution to offensive speech has long been 'more speech, not enforced silence'.

But while it may be the best available response to noxious expression, counterspeech is an imperfect solution. It can lead to a 'heckler's veto', whereby voices protesting speech are themselves so loud and overpowering that the original speaker cannot be heard, and those in the audience lose their right to listen. The right to hear speech is itself an element of free expression that is recognised under the First Amendment and in international law. In early 2024 PEN America hosted an event in Los Angeles with two speakers, one of whom – comedian and actress Mayim Bialik – was a frequent commentator on the Israel–Hamas war. The topic of the conversation was a personal memoir unrelated to the Israel–Hamas conflict. The event protocols, which allowed for protest up until the point when it violated the rights of other speakers and

listeners, were announced before the proceedings began. When a small group of protesters targeting Bialik began playing an audio recording of the names of individuals who had been killed in Gaza, organisers allowed the audio feed for a few minutes and then asked the demonstrators to stop. They did, briefly, but then restarted at a louder volume, making it impossible for the onstage event to be heard. The protesters were then asked to leave, and five out of the six did so voluntarily. The sixth, who was holding the amplifier, continued the disruption. Venue security staff slid her chair out of the room to allow the event to proceed as planned, managing to do so without touching her physically. Online critics accused PEN America of interfering with the protester's speech rights. It was understandably upsetting for the individual protester to be pulled out of the event; it was not a situation we relished, nor one we had faced in more than ten years of hosting frequent public programmes. We sympathised with the protesters' effort to draw attention to the horrific suffering in Gaza. But in replying to critics we stressed that the protest, if allowed to continue, would have denied the expressive rights of hundreds of others – both on stage and in the audience. It would have been a classic

demonstration of the 'heckler's veto' where the loudest voice drowns out those of others.

As renowned First Amendment scholars Howard Gillman and Erwin Chemerinsky have written, 'it has long been recognized in constitutional law that the "heckler's veto" – defined as the suppression of speech in order to appease disruptive, hostile, or threatening members of the audience – can be as much a threat to rights of free expression as government censorship.'[35] Some argued that a message about civilian deaths in Gaza should take priority over any other expression. Others claimed that Bialik's views disqualified her from speaking and meant that she somehow forfeited expressive rights. But if the premise is that individual audience-goers wield the power to override the priorities of event organisers and invited speakers, it is easy to imagine who would ultimately be silenced. Well-resourced corporate interests could drown out critics, white supremacists could shout down racial justice advocates, and majorities of nativists could prevent immigrants from being heard. As Gillman and Chemerinsky have pointed out, 'the idea that private individuals cannot censor what the government is required to protect played a vitally important role during the civil-rights movement,

when courts prevented officials in the South from stopping speeches and marches based on the threat of hostile audiences'. Without such rules and parameters governing individual speech, free speech for society as a whole is compromised.

The power of the heckler's veto is not limited to the room in which the disruption takes place. In the spring of 2024 in the United States, scores of events – commencement ceremonies, convocations and lectures – were cancelled amid demonstrations over the Israel–Hamas conflict, often for vaguely cited 'security reasons'. These shut-downs were prompted by fear of the spectacle and the viral video that might result from a potential disruption. Campuses and conveners knew that if they allowed a heckler to derail their event they would be rebuked for sacrificing the rights and interests of many for those of the loudest and most intransigent. But to throw protesters out, especially by force, could fuel a backlash in the form of even more vociferous protests. In instances where events were pre-emptively cancelled, the hecklers got their veto without ever having to say a word.

The heckler's veto is not the only risk associated with counterspeech. In an ideal, imaginary system, the consequences of speech would be

proportionate to the hurt and offence caused. An attentive parent might penalise a child for obnoxious or insensitive speech through a calibrated retort, lecture or punishment. Their aim would be to exact a reprisal commensurate to the crime: a mild insult to a sibling might elicit a stern word; an unprovoked taunt towards a neighbour might warrant a firm talking-to and loss of privileges; the bullying of a child on the basis of race or disability could warrant a severe punishment and steps to ensure such conduct did not recur. The parent would be careful to take account of the child's intent: was their remark laced with hostility, or just an innocent comment that landed badly? Should they have known better, or did they inadvertently blunder into an offence that – perhaps because of their age – they could not have been expected to foresee? They would also consider the context: was the comment made in a moment of extreme stress or upset? Should they have realised that the offensive remark would be heard by the person who was hurt by it? A parent would carefully assess those factors in determining what consequences for the speech were warranted.

A school or university administration would ideally carry out a version of the same analysis,

looking at what rules were violated and what circumstances should shape an appropriate institutional response. In either setting, individuals in positions of authority would contemplate how to react so as to disincentivise future offence. But they would also aim not to *overreact* to the point where the child or the student, and their peers, would live in fear that an inadvertent or minor speech infraction could land them in serious trouble. They would strive for an outcome that would be seen as fair, or relatively so, by all sides. They would also consider the knock-on effects of their decision, trying to create incentives that set boundaries clearly without excessively chilling speech.

In an open, digitised and boundaryless marketplace of ideas, and particularly one that is algorithmically powered, there is no such calibration. There is no single sage who determines the right collective response to speech in the public square. Instead, hundreds, thousands or even millions of people individually encounter speech and react, often without even fully reading or viewing the content that riles them up. Online, there are incentives to respond; having your tweet or post liked or shared can feel validating. You can express solidarity that deepens your relationships or stature within

a group. You can dash off a retort that helps release your own frustration or anger. A pithy rejoinder or potent video can help amass new followers whom you may be able to monetise. The overwhelming proportion of online engagement occurs within minutes and hours of a post, meaning that if you don't react fast, the moment will pass. Those factors can all contribute to a thunderous drumbeat of counterspeech, making even remotely controversial speech so risky that it just doesn't seem worth the potential price.

The problem is not just online. The digital realm has also become an amplification chamber for speech in the physical world – a snippet from a classroom discussion or lecture can be shared for all the world to hear, and call out. When those involved are in some way notable or the speech is shocking, the incident can get picked up by the media, further raising the temperature. Encounters at stores, on planes and in parks go viral, with sometimes life-altering consequences. Paradoxically, while everyone involved is doing nothing more than exercising their free speech rights, the net result can be profoundly inimical to freewheeling discourse.

The problem becomes even more acute when public outrage forces the hand of authorities and

institutions to punish speech that, absent such reverberating outcry, might be met with a more measured response. In March 2020, the staff of Hachette USA were up in arms over the book publisher's decision to put out a memoir by film-maker Woody Allen, objecting that he had been the subject of serious allegations of child abuse. Although these had never legally been proven, the company's leadership felt compelled to capitulate to demands that were ricocheting across social media and had made it into the *New York Times*. The executives cancelled the book, a decision that a Hachette leader later said they regretted. The swell of online outrage can rattle not just the target of opprobrium, but anyone linked to it. As those associated with an institution – such as employees or members – come to feel embarrassed or publicly pressured over something that has caused offence, they can tighten the screws on higher-ups who hold decision-making power. The impetus to get out of the digital line of fire is potent and can prompt precipitous moves just to quell the uproar.

Even when institutions feel they have no choice but to submit to outcry and cancel speakers or books, the decision-makers bear prime responsibility for the decision to suppress and also chill

speech. Publishers should resist popular demands to abandon controversial books, insisting on the value of making available a diverse array of content that may interest – and sometimes offend – varied constituencies. When they withstand public or staff pressure to pull or repudiate a book, publishers not only stand up for a single book, but also send a message that capitulation is not the only viable response to furore. Universities should, likewise, stand by their decisions to host controversial speakers and accept that uproar may ensue. University graduations that went forward in the spring of 2024 often included some disruption, but not so much that graduates and their families were denied the chance to hear out speakers and to celebrate.

There is often little sympathy for individual speakers whose provocative or objectionable statements or social media posts get them into hot water. They may be derided as blundering, artless or wilfully provocative. But incidents in which swelling outrage over speech results in humiliation and even cancellation reverberate beyond the individual speaker. They are public spectacles that put everyone watching on notice that if they transgress someone's notion of appropriate expressive boundaries, they may meet the same fate: humiliation,

ostracisation and a loss of opportunity. That collective lesson, in turn, reshapes the whole landscape for free speech, resetting – and narrowing – the bounds of what can be said.

A necessary corollary to the notion that freedom of speech must not mean freedom from consequences is thus the idea that our freedom to exact consequences must not be so absolute as to negate free speech entirely. By veering into threats and intimidation, including doxing, counterspeakers bring to bear repercussions that chill speech. Calls for official punishment of speech that has not broken any written rules can also deter open expression. Forcefully rejecting or even condemning speech need not entail a demand that the speaker suffer reprisal for what they have said. Even if a speaker or their message is unappealing, ostracisation can cross into demonisation, dehumanisation and sometimes even death threats. Harassment campaigns, the targeting of family members, and invasions of personal privacy in the name of delivering a message foreclose dialogue and exchange. While this may be warranted in response to rank bigotry or support for violence, short of that, such virulent reprisals for the voicing of a disfavoured opinion debase the wider culture.

This doesn't mean all counterspeech must be civil or temperate. Some disruption – intermittent heckling, a stinging rebuttal online – can power-fully make a point. Part of the intention of protest is to rattle and challenge a speaker or institution; rules cannot be so strict as to make that effect-ively impossible. There are also potent ways to protest – including walkouts, banners, marches and die-ins – that don't trammel the speech rights of others or ride roughshod over reasonable rules.

Online it is tempting to vilify and seek to extin-guish anything that affronts us. But doing so legit-imises mobs to exert a power that laws deny to elected government officials: the authority to decide what ideas live and die in the public sphere. A good test is whether the ferocity of counterspeech and protest against ideas you loathe would seem justi-fied if mounted against ideas you agree with, but others reject. Should an encampment demanding the right of white men not to have their opportun-ities circumscribed by affirmative action be permit-ted in the college square? What about a pro-Putin protest that disrupted classes and made Ukrainian students feel fearful? Exacting consequences for speech can be empowering, but Justice Brandeis championed counterspeech not to gratify the

speaker but to advance the truth. Ultimately, the purpose of counterspeech should not be to punish or humiliate, but to persuade.

A related argument against free speech protections is that they reinforce the power of those in positions of strength and suppress the ability of the disenfranchised to challenge authority and even upend power structures. History and present-day experience indicate otherwise. Codified liberal free speech protections transcend politics and ideology, protecting everyone irrespective of their position in life or their political leanings. In practice they can, of course, be invoked to safeguard the rights of the privileged, those aligned with the government or those seeking to perpetuate the subordination of other groups. Protections for hate speech can be invoked to protect white supremacist groups for speech that denigrates but falls short of the threshold for harassment or a true threat. But free speech safeguards are also essential for shielding speech that confronts, criticises and even incenses those in power – climate activism, campus protests for divestment from Israel, transgender rights, immigration reform and more. In fact, those challenging the powerful have the most to gain from free speech protections because they are at the greatest

risk of being targeted for retaliation by those with the force and resources to do so, whether through legal means, public shaming or otherwise. In practice, in the United States, the major twentieth-century Supreme Court rulings that defined and expanded the scope of First Amendment protections virtually all dealt with left-wing dissidents challenging government power and decisions: war resisters and protesters, labour organisers, communists, historically excluded religious groups and political dissidents. In authoritarian countries it is authors, opposition leaders, investigative journalists and human rights defenders who sit in prison; their confinement a warning signal to others who might dare challenge the government.

Major civil rights leaders recognised the centrality of free speech protections to the struggles they were waging, with Frederick Douglass famously saying on the eve of the Civil War in 1860 that 'thrones, dominions, principalities, and powers, founded in injustice and wrong, are sure to tremble, if men are allowed to reason of righteousness, temperance, and of a judgement to come in their presence. Slavery cannot tolerate free speech. Five years of its exercise would banish the auction block and break every chain in the South.'[36] Over a century

later, Martin Luther King similarly highlighted the centrality of free speech to American culture and to the struggles he was waging during the final address of his life, known as the 'I've Been to the Mountaintop' speech, delivered the day before he was assassinated: 'If I lived in China or even Russia, or any totalitarian country, maybe I could understand . . . the denial of certain basic First Amendment privileges, because they haven't committed themselves to that over there. But somewhere I read of the freedom of assembly. Somewhere I read of the freedom of speech. Somewhere I read of the freedom of press. Somewhere I read that the greatness of America is the right to protest for right. And so just as I say, we aren't going to let dogs or water hoses turn us around, we aren't going to let any injunction turn us around. We are going on.'[37]

Some critics of free speech discourse argue that its principles fail to account for power differentials. They might claim, for example, that the speech of an adjunct lecturer or even a heckler warrants greater protection if they are a voice of the marginalised, whereas those speaking for the majority or the monied can legitimately be hemmed in when necessary in service of other societal interests. But power is not static enough, nor uniformly

understood enough, to make it a workable general exception to free speech precepts. In a May 2024 essay on the US campus protests, author Zadie Smith pointed out that while the pro-Palestine demonstrators saw themselves as the voice of powerless innocents targeted in Gaza, 'within the ethical zone of interest that is a campus, which was not so long ago defined as a safe space, delineated by the boundary of a generation's ethical ideas – *it may well be* that a Jewish student walking past the tents, who finds herself referred to as a Zionist, and then is warned to keep her distance, is, in that moment, the weakest participant in the zone. If the concept of safety is foundational to these students' ethical philosophy (as I take it to be), and, if the protests are committed to reinserting ethical principles into a cynical and corrupt politics, it is not right to divest from these same ethics at the very moment they come into conflict with other imperatives.'[38] While it is certainly true that power relations shape the landscape for free speech, the protections need to be nimble enough to account for shifts and subtleties in power relations. Recent debates have demonstrated how the language of harm, powerlessness and vulnerability can be used as both sword and shield. Book ban proponents

have talked about psychological safety in relation to young children who may be exposed to stories about sensitive subjects of gender and race. Conservative voices who believe their ideas are frozen out of the academy can describe themselves as marginalised or powerless.

Present-day attacks on books featuring diverse characters, and on curricula on subjects including race and gender and other hot button topics, illustrate both the propensity of those in positions of power to police and suppress speech they disagree with, and also the importance of legal and cultural bulwarks in defence of free speech to stand in their way. In 2023 PEN America and a group of partners filed a lawsuit in Escambia County, Florida challenging the removal of thousands of books from the countywide school system.[39] The books in question fit the national pattern for such bans, with most involving stories covering race, gender and sexuality, subjects some parents might regard as controversial. In overruling the Escambia County government's motion to dismiss our case, the judge, a conservative Trump appointee, relied on First Amendment precedent to find 'that school officials cannot remove books solely because they disagree with the views expressed in the books'. If the First

Amendment text and subsequent case law did not curtail the government's leeway in this respect, then specific books could and likely would have been permanently removed at the behest of county officials. This would interfere with authors' ability to reach audiences and kids' chance to choose what to read. In this and countless other examples, free speech precepts are invoked in order to protect the rights of historically marginalised groups.

As social critiques and campaigns are mounted, their leaders should take a page from past progressive icons like Douglass and King in ensuring that their supporters recognise the centrality of free speech to their ability to contest conventional wisdom and confront those in power. Unfortunately, certain contemporary social movements have lost sight of the imperative of free speech safeguards, as well as their universality. They have called for punishments of speech that offends them, arguing that it causes intolerable hurt or harm. Yet such demands, particularly when directed at institutions, reinforce the notion that those in positions of institutional and legal power rightly possess the authority to police speech on the basis of viewpoint, acting as gatekeepers for the bounds of permissible discourse.

The first step to recovery is admitting there is a problem. There are early signs that recent events are leading US universities to face up to concerns about a shrinking environment for unfettered debate and heterodox thinking on campus, and to contemplate some major reforms. In late May 2024 Harvard University announced a decision to avoid public pronouncements on issues not relating directly to the university's mission, an effort to avoid being seen to take a stance on social issues.[40] Several recent decisions from US courts hearing lawsuits challenging book bans and related restrictions suggest that even conservative jurists recognise that such measures may run afoul of the First Amendment. Even Florida Governor Ron DeSantis, the sponsor and champion of laws restricting teaching and learning on issues of race and sexual orientation, has now acknowledged that policies empowering any citizen to challenge the availability of any book in Florida schools and get it withdrawn from shelves go too far. Constituencies on the left and the right may be slowly waking up to the risk of free speech being undermined as a bedrock constitutional and societal value. They may finally be beginning to recognise how the erosion of free speech as a norm will encroach on their own leeway

to express themselves. The alarm bells are ringing. It is time to rise up in response to the erosion of respect for free speech, and activate a constituency ready and equipped to defend it.

Mobilising for free speech does not mean calling open season for hateful expression, nor wishing away the concerns of those who point out that speech has consequences and can cause hurt or, sometimes, even harm. The defence of free speech in the twenty-first century must take account of the imperatives of equality and inclusivity, principles that are essential for a thriving pluralistic democracy predicated on liberal values. But the embrace of those principles needs, and must not come at the expense of, free speech. Open discourse cannot flourish in a world where all must hold their tongues lest they say something construed as contradicting ideals of diversity and equity.

An urgent, forthright reckoning with the precarious place of free speech in the twenty-first century is essential to ensuring that the campuses, public squares, online platforms and even courthouses of the future do not turn their backs on it in the name of other values. It is vital that rising generations recognise the centrality of it to the causes they care about, the movements they are building,

SUZANNE NOSSEL

and the communities they want to inhabit. In the decades to come it will fall to those generations to defend and develop free speech principles that are fit for purpose in a fast-evolving society. To carry out that responsibility, today's young people need to be grounded in why free speech matters, what it makes possible and what is lost when it is eroded. Those who care about free speech cannot leave it to be misunderstood, politicised, weaponised or abandoned. To safeguard free speech for future generations demands a searching examination of how free speech is threatened and urgent action to shore it up.

Turn this book over to read the alternative view.

Notes

1. Katherine Knott, '4 More Colleges Face Civil Rights Investigations', *Inside Higher Ed*, 18 January 2024: https://www.insidehighered.com/news/government/2024/01/18/u-minnesota-four-others-facing-new-civil-rights-probes
2. Vanessa Clarke, 'Free-speech tsar Arif Ahmed set to defend all views', BBC News, 1 June 2023: https://www.bbc.com/news/education-65776173
3. Hélène de Lauzun, 'New French Law Destroys Freedom of Private Speech', *European Conservative*, 12 March 2024: https://europeanconservative.com/articles/commentary/new-french-law-destroys-freedom-of-private-speech/
4. Loveday Morris and Kate Brady, 'In Germany's struggle against antisemitism, the arts are suffering', *Washington Post*, 22 December 2023: https://www.washingtonpost.com/world/2023/12/22/germany-antisemitism-israel-gaza-arts-censorship/
5. Bobby Allyn, 'TikTok challenges U.S. ban in court, calling it unconstitutional', NPR, 7 May 2024: https://www.npr.org/2024/05/07/1246532784/tiktok-ban-us-court-biden-congress
6. 'Halloween Costume Controversy', FIRE, n.d.: https://www.thefire.org/research-learn/halloween-costume-controversy

7. Maeve Duggan, 'The Demographics of Social Media Users', Pew Research Center, 19 August 2015: https://www.pewresearch.org/internet/2015/08/19/the-demographics-of-social-media-users/

8. 'Survey: Half of U.S. College Students "Intimidated" When Sharing Views', Buckley Institute, 26 October 2015: https://buckleyinstitute.com/survey-half-of-u-s-college-students-intimidated-when-sharing-views/

9. Greg Lukianoff and Jonathan Haidt, 'The Coddling of the American Mind', *The Atlantic*, September 2015: https://www.theatlantic.com/magazine/archive/2015/09/the-coddling-of-the-american-mind/399356/

10. Cat Zakrzewski, 'White House announces tech company efforts to combat violent extremism', *Washington Post*, 15 September 2022: https://www.washingtonpost.com/technology/2022/09/15/white-house-tech-extremism/

11. Walter Mosley, 'Why I Quit the Writers' Room', *New York Times*, 6 September 2019: https://www.nytimes.com/2019/09/06/opinion/sunday/walter-mosley.html

12. Suzanne Nossel, 'You can only protect campus speech if you acknowledge racism', *Washington Post*, 25 May 2018: https://www.washingtonpost.com/outlook/you-can-only-protect-campus-speech-if-you-acknowledge-racism/2018/05/25/5c26bbcc-59ed-11e8-b656-a5f8c2a9295d_story.html

13. Samantha Harris, 'Unconstitutional "Bias Reporting" Programs: A Nationwide Problem', FIRE, 29 November, 2007: https://www.thefire.org/news/unconstitutional-bias-reporting-programs-nationwide-problem

14. Anemona Hartocollis, 'M.I.T. Will No Longer Require Diversity Statements for Hiring Faculty', *New York Times*, 6 May 2024: https://www.nytimes.com/2024/05/06/us/mit-diversity-statements-faculty-hiring.html

15. Myriam Gurba, 'Pendeja, You Ain't Steinbeck: My Bronca with Fake-Ass Social Justice Literature', *Tropics of Meta*, 12 December 2019: https://tropicsofmeta. com/2019/12/12/pendeja-you-aint-steinbeck-my-bronca-with-fake-ass-social-justice-literature/

16. Daniel A. Olivas, 'Yes, Latinx writers are angry about American Dirt- and we will not be silent', *The Guardian*, 30 January 2020: https://www.theguardian.com/ commentisfree/2020/jan/30/american-dirt-book-controversy-latinx-writers-angry

17. Parul Sehgal, 'A Mother and Son, Fleeing for Their Lives Over Treacherous Terrain', *New York Times*, 17 January 2020: https://www.nytimes.com/2020/01/17/books/ review-american-dirt-jeanine-cummins.html

18. James Tager and Clarisse Rosaz Sharif, 'Reading Between the Lines: Race, Equity, and Book Publishing', PEN America, 17 October 2022: https://pen.org/report/ race-equity-and-book-publishing/

19. 'Booklash: Literary Freedom, Online Outrage, and the Language of Harm', PEN America, 7 August 2023: https://pen.org/report/booklash/

20. Niraj Chokshi, 'What College Students Really Think About Free Speech', *New York Times*, 12 March 2018: https://www.nytimes.com/2018/03/12/us/college-students-free-speech.html

21. Jeannie Suk Gersen, 'The Trouble with Teaching Rape Law', *New Yorker*, 15 December 2014: https:// newyorker.com/news/news-desk/trouble-teaching-rape-law

22. 'Free Expression on College Campuses', College Pulse, May 2019: https://kf-site-production.s3.amazonaws. com/media_elements/files/000/000/351/original/ Knight-CP-Report-FINAL.pdf

23. Sungjoo Yoon, 'I'm a High School Junior. Let's Talk About "Huckleberry Finn" and "Mockingbird"', *New York Times*, 18 April 2022: https://www.nytimes.com/2022/04/18/opinion/school-book-bans-students.html

24. 'A Letter on Justice and Open Debate', *Harper's*, 7 July 2020: https://harpers.org/a-letter-on-justice-and-open-debate/

25. 'A More Specific Letter on Justice and Open Debate', *The Objective*, 10 July 2020: https://objectivejournalism.org/2020/07/a-more-specific-letter-on-justice-and-open-debate/

26. 'Educational Gag Orders Target Speech about LGBTQ+ Identities with New Prohibitions and Punishments', PEN America, 15 February 2022: https://pen.org/educational-gag-orders-target-speech-about-lgbtq-identities-with-new-prohibitions-and-punishments/

27. Sabrina Baêta and Kasey Meehan, 'Spineless Shelves: Two Years of Book Banning', PEN America, 14 December 2023: https://pen.org/spineless-shelves/

28. Sean Stevens, '2024 College Free Speech Rankings: What Is the State of Free Speech on America's College Campuses?', FIRE, 6 September 2023: https://www.thefire.org/sites/default/files/2023/09/CFSR%202024_final_updated.pdf

29. 'National Speech Index – April 2024 Topline Results', FIRE, 8 May 2024: https://www.thefire.org/research-learn/national-speech-index-april-2024-topline-results

30. The *New York Times* Editorial Board, 'America Has a Free Speech Problem', *New York Times*, 18 March 2022: https://www.nytimes.com/2022/03/18/opinion/cancel-culture-free-speech-poll.html

31. The *Crimson* Editorial Board, 'Some Cautious Counsel to the Academic Freedom Council', *Harvard Crimson*, 1 May 2023: https://www.thecrimson.com/article/2023/5/1/editorial-harvard-academic-freedom-council

32. 'PEN International Charter', PEN America, 1948: https://pen.org/pen-charter/

33. Zachary Small, 'Indiana University Cancels Major Exhibition of Palestinian Artist', *New York Times*, 11 January 2024: https://www.nytimes.com/2024/01/11/arts/design/indiana-university-samia-halaby-exhibition-canceled.html

34. 'Online Harassment Field Manual', PEN America, 20 April 2018: https://onlineharassmentfieldmanual.pen.org/

35. Howard Gillman and Erwin Chemerinsky, 'Does Disruption Violate Free Speech?', *Chronicle of Higher Education*, 17 October 2017: https://www.chronicle.com/article/does-disruption-violate-free-speech/

36. Frederick Douglass, 'A Plea for Freedom of Speech in Boston', Tremont Temple Baptist Church, Boston, Massachusetts, 3 December 1860. Transcript. The Constitution Center: https://constitutioncenter.org/education/classroom-resource-library/classroom/10.5-primary-source-frederick-douglass-plea-for-freedom-of-speech-in-boston

37. Martin Luther King Jr., '"I've Been to the Mountaintop"', Mason Temple, Memphis, Tennessee, 3 April 1968. Transcript. American RadioWorks: https://americanradioworks.publicradio.org/features/blackspeech/mlkingjr.html

38. Zadie Smith, 'Shibboleth', *New Yorker*, 5 May |2024: https://www.newyorker.com/news/essay/shibboleth-the-role-of-words-in-the-campus-protests

39. 'PEN America v. Escambia County School District', PEN America, 31 January 2024: https://pen.org/pen-america-v-escambia-county/

40. Emma H. Haidar and Cam E. Kettles, 'Harvard Will Refrain From Controversial Statements About Public Policy Issues', *Harvard Crimson*, 28 May 2024: https://www.thecrimson.com/article/2024/5/28/harvard-institutional-neutrality-report/